Why Are the Heroes Always White?

columns by

Sheryl McCarthy

New York Newsday

ANDREWS AND McMEEL
A Universal Press Syndicate Company
Kansas City

To Len Hollie and Gladys and Lorenza McCarthy

Additional copies of this book may be ordered by calling (800) 642–6480.

Library of Congress Cataloging-in-Publication Data

McCarthy, Sheryl.
    Why are the heroes always white? : columns / by Sheryl McCarthy.
      p.   cm.
  ISBN 0-8362-7049-5
    1. Afro-Americans—New York (N.Y.)—Social conditions.
2. New York (N.Y.)—Social conditions. I. Title.
F128.9.N3M33   1995
305.89'6073—dc20

                                                        94-49059
                                                         CIP

Designed by Barrie Maguire

Contents

CHAPTER FOUR: **No books, no brains, no chance**

CHAPTER FIVE: **What's up with this? Young and in trouble**

CHAPTER SIX: **Why are the heroes always white?**

CHAPTER SEVEN: **Lawmakers, heartbreakers**

CHAPTER EIGHT: **New York stories: The garden is still green**

Acknowledgments

I would like to thank Jim Toedtman and Donald Forst, editors of *New York Newsday*, who thrust the idea of writing a column into my head when I wasn't sure I really wanted to do it or had anything to say in a column.

I also thank Les Payne, whose high standards of what a columnist should be, and of what the responsibilities of a black columnist are, have spurred me to reconsider how I approach my own column.

I especially thank Mort Persky, who edits my column. His even temper and kind disposition make him a joy to work with, and his astute suggestions and gentle prodding have often resulted in columns that are much better than they were when I originally wrote them.

Finally, I thank Bob Heisler, whose idea it was to publish this collection of my columns, and who did most of the hard work of going through the files and pulling them together and editing them.

Introduction

When I was growing up I used to dream of becoming a great fiction writer. I remember crying over Harper Lee's novel, *To Kill a Mockingbird,* a novel about a young girl like me, growing up in Alabama in the days before the civil rights movement changed the demeaning way whites treated blacks in the South. I vowed that one day I too would write stories with such power and poignancy.

By the time I'd been out of college a few years, my dream of writing fiction had begun to recede. I was having too much fun covering daily news events as a journalist. The personalities and human dramas I encountered in the course of doing my stories were so compelling they replaced any need to create fictional characters.

Being a journalist is fun. It amazes me that because I write for a newspaper, people who are total strangers will let me into their homes and tell me their most intimate secrets. Having this entree to people I would otherwise never meet and to places I would otherwise never see has been the most rewarding part of being a journalist.

When I first became a columnist a few years ago, my female friends told me I should "go after the men." My black friends urged me to "go after the whites." This was understandable in a business where almost all the columnists had heretofore been white males, many of whom shared a similar view of the world, especially when it came to judging people who did not look like themselves.

But I realized I didn't want to go after the men or the whites particularly, but simply to write what I felt about the things I cared about and to try to tell the truth about people and events as I saw it.

I see my job as a columnist as sorting through the passions and emotions, the political machinations, the lies and the hyperbole that often surround events and to find out where the truth lies. It's also my job to restore balance to the way stories are reported, whether it's to offer a woman's perspective to the male writers' view of the world or to inject a black person's perspective into the white writers' take on things.

Black people are often dehumanized in the news-stereotyped as criminals and lethargic welfare mothers and victims or perpetrators of one pathology or another. I try to write about them as I know them, conveying the nobility and complexity of their lives as well as their problems and struggles.

The title of this book comes from one of the very first columns I ever wrote. It was about the Howard Beach case, a notorious incident in which some white guys in Queens beat up and chased some black guys who happened to come into their neighborhood. One black man, Michael Griffiths, was chased into the path of an oncoming car and was killed.

Some months later I heard that a TV drama based on the trial of the white guys was about to be shown. The ad promoting the show talked about the white prosecutor of the case in glowing terms, saying "he was the only one who could bring the guilty to justice." This was typical of the way stories about black people are portrayed on television and in the movies. The blacks are always the passive spectators to the events of their own lives; the whites are always the heroes.

"Why are the heroes always white?" I asked my editor, musing over a column I was going to write on the subject. He said I should make that the opening sentence of my column. I did, and it is also the title of the chapter in this book about race relations.

I once knew a columnist who regarded the world as a battleground, with everyone out to get him. I envisaged him getting up the morning and fighting his way out of bed and into and out of the shower. I could just see him fighting his way into his clothes and fighting his way out the door of his apartment to the world outside. Then he battled his way through the crowds on the subway and in the streets and into the office. Once in the office, he fought his way through the reporters and editors who he felt were out to get him. Not surprisingly, his column reflected this siegelike mentality.

My view of the world is more benign and I think my columns reflect that. What angers me is abuse and exploitation and most of all people who use dishonesty and deception to manipulate others for their own benefit.

I consider myself privileged to have grown up in Birmingham, Ala., and to have lived through the civil rights movement. The black people who fought this battle were among the noblest and most courageous people I have ever known.

I am also lucky that New York City has been my home, off and on, for twenty years. Its energy and the resilience and humor—as well as the sometimes bad behavior of its people—still fascinates me.

One of the good things about going from a reporter to being a columnist is that people who never noticed your byline before suddenly recognize who you are and start caring about what you say. You go from being a faceless name on a story to being a real person, and people whom you've never met start walking up to you on the street and talking to you like an old friend.

The very best part of being a columnist, however, is being able to touch a nerve in others-to make my readers angry or sad, to make them think about events differently, or to express something they have been feeling, but have been unable to express.

Right after Operation Desert Storm, I wrote a column that questioned the true motives of the United States for invading Iraq, versus the public relations spin the government was putting on the story. One day a man stopped me on the street and asked me if I was "that newspaper writer." When I said yes, he told me he and his co-workers had been passing my column around the office that day.

"You said exactly what I was thinking but didn't know how to say," he told me.

This is as good as it gets and it's the best reason I know for getting up in the morning and writing a column.

Sheryl McCarthy

Chapter 1

"Where does Sheryl McCarthy get off writing about black people, when she's Irish?"

Hello, Uncle Kilty!

JULY 11, 1990

Every so often I get letters in the mail inviting me to buy assorted paraphernalia of the McCarthy clan.

I've been offered an oil painting, suitable for framing, of the original Blarney Castle in County Kerry, Ireland, the ancestral home of the McCarthys. I could also purchase the McCarthy coat of arms reproduced on parchment-like paper, or a book of true stories about famous McCarthys through the ages, including MacCarthy Mor, that fearless 15th-century chieftain who refused to surrender his ancestral powers to the British throne.

A few years ago I was even invited to attend the Great Reunion of the McCarthys in Ireland. I actually toyed with the idea of going. I had visions of running up to a ruddy-faced man in his 60s, enclosing him in a bear hug and exclaiming, "Uncle Kilty, I'm so happy to see you! I'm your long-lost niece."

I find the barrage of McCarthy paraphernalia all the more amusing since I am a black American who grew up in the Deep South. In that region, which is only a few generations removed from slavery, I would often ruminate about how I came to be a black person with an Irish name. On the one hand, being a McCarthy strengthened my emotional tie to Scarlett O'Hara, that fiery, ambitious southern heroine who was descended from another of the great Irish clans. On the other hand, not all my feelings about having a white name were that pleasant.

Most American blacks bear the names of white slaveowners who were Irish, British, Scotch, French, Polish, or whatever, who passed their names along to their human property. Often they passed along their genes as well, since, despite laws against racial intermingling, the slavemasters did a lot of dallying outside their race.

The extent of this commingling is evident in the brown to white skin tones of many black people, and in the names they carry. Like my friend Freeman Hrabowski, who throughout our childhood carried a Polish name that few black people in our community could pronounce. His family got its name from white slaveholders in Lowndes County, Ala., and he has great-aunts and uncles who, with their light skin and straight hair, look like they could be of Polish descent. To this day there are a number of white people running around Lowndes County who are related to him.

My family presumably takes its name from a southern slave owner, although none of my relatives seem to know which McCarthy he was or where he lived. We only know he was Irish.

Then there's my friend George Muchita. When I first met George I wondered how a black person got a Japanese name. It turns out Muchita is not Japanese, but French, as in *moo-shee-tah*, that his father is Carlton Bouvier Muchita from Virginia, and that George's ancestors were French.

"A lot of people take me to be Chinese or Hispanic when we talk on the telephone," George says. "When they see me in person this expression comes across their faces, one of sheer shock!"

Blacks in this country often shy away from their geneal-ogies. I think it's because reconstructing the family tree con-jures images of slavery and oppression, of the master sneaking into the slave quarters for a bit of forced socializing. I am reminded of just how universal this commingling is whenever I see black South Africans who visit this country. While most Africans are dark-skinned, most of the South Africans I've seen are medium brown. It is interesting that in a country where racial segregation was so rigidly enforced there is so much interracial socializing going on.

Black Americans all know we're not racially pure. But whites, who've clearly been as involved in this fraternization as we have, rarely entertain the idea that the gene pool is so mixed. I figure if white genes have made their way into our gene pool, surely a few stray black genes made their way over the fence. Could this possibly explain why a singer like Michael McDonald sings in the same husky tones as Ray Charles, or how Elvis got that twitch in his hips?

Two other anecdotes on this theme bear telling. One is about my grandmother, a brown-skinned woman from rural Alabama who was born Lillie Jackson. In her youth she fell in love with and married a man named Ernest White, thereby becoming Lillie White, the name she bore for the rest of her life.

The other story is about the time I wrote a newspaper article that provoked an angry phone call from an irate black reader. "Where does Sheryl McCarthy get off writing about black people," she complained, "when she's Irish?"

In a time when everything from rapes in the park to shootouts in the street seems to polarize us along racial lines, the extent to which we are all intertwined bears thinking about. As the experience of the McCarthy family proves, we are all in this together, and it's high time we started behaving that way.

Betrayal Still Aches

JUNE 26, 1991

Since the black revolution of the 1960s and '70s, black women have repeatedly heard themselves celebrated. They are strong. They are dynamic. They are smart. They are resourceful. They are loving. They are beautiful daughters of the Nile.

They hear this from everyone: from black men, white men, from white women feminists who marvel at their resilience. This image of strong black womanhood is rooted in slavery times. It is the image of the slave woman who could bear a child in the morning and be back working in the cotton fields by afternoon.

But black women realize what this myth really means: that being strong usually translates into doing it all by yourself. More than 60 percent of all black households in this country are headed by a woman, whether she's a single mother raising children on welfare or a corporate executive fighting the corporate battles of racism and sexism.

In his movie, *Jungle Fever*, Spike Lee gives us a glimpse of black women's anger. It appears to be anger over interracial dating. But that's only part of the story. It is also anger over the double-speak that celebrates black women, but then lets them down—hard.

Start with the waitress at the Harlem restaurant who turns

evil when Flipper Purify, a young black architect, brings his white secretary and girlfriend to dinner. "You tired, brother," she tells him, acidly. "I can't believe you brought this stringy-haired _____ here to eat!"

Cut to the raging Drew Purify, Flipper's wife, who learns about his affair and then throws Flipper, his clothes and his architect's tools out of the house. "Explain the _____ white bitch, you _____," Drew screams as she throws his clothes onto the sidewalk. Then there's the famous war council scene, in which Drew is consoled by her girlfriends. These black women vent their frustrations about many things: about black men's betraying them for white women, about a standard of beauty that undervalues them, about the overall man short-age—about the frustration of finding themselves somewhere between a rock and a hard place. Their conversation is filled with anger, sarcasm, wit—and ultimately, sadness. Drew starts off feeling humiliated because her husband has left her—an attractive, educated, clothes buyer at Bloomingdale's—for a working-class white woman from Bensonhurst. But her anger quickly fades into sorrow. "It don't even matter what color she is," she says finally. "My man is gone."

Much has been made of the anger of black men, of the racial oppression that robs them of a livelihood or of the oppor-tunity for professional advancement; the oppression that ren-ders them unable to support their families and gnaws at their self-respect. The theme is that black men suffer worst from racism, since they're men, after all, who are out there on the firing line, and have such sensitive psyches.

But black women are angry too. For one thing, they know that they aren't really considered beautiful. "Do any of you know what it is like not being considered attractive?" asks one of Drew Purify's darker-skinned girlfriends. She goes on to tell about how all the desirable men she knew pursued women with white features and straight hair.

In fact, in the movie, the only black women who have men are the light-skinned ones. When Drew, the fairest of them all, loses her husband to a white woman, it's the ultimate insult.

When I was in college I was constantly amazed by the black militants, the guys with dashikis and shark-tooth necklaces and overgrown Afros, the guys who demanded revolution and denounced everything white. Invariably, they were the ones whose wives or girlfriends were white. Black might be beautiful in theory—but in practice, white was better. In contrast, most white men simply don't view black women as dating or marriage material. For them, black women exist on two planes. She's either a marvel, a star, and an icon—or she's a whore or a servant. She is rarely anything in between. I've heard white guys fantasize about the likes of a Robin Givens or a Lola Falana, but they can't relate to the black woman down the hall. A few, like Paulie in the movie, will attempt to engage a black woman on a personal level. But most do not.

Black men expect black women to be strong. They expect her to hold a job, raise the children, absorb his pain as well as deal with her own. They expect her to be loyal, not just on a personal but on a racial level. So when, like Flipper Purify, a black man leaves a black woman for a white one, it's more than just philandering. It feels like betrayal.

A friend of mine put it best. "It's not just that Flipper's gone off with a white woman so much as it is that he's just plain gone," she said. "The problem is there's nobody, black, white or other, to take his place."

I personally have nothing against interracial relationships. I think people should date and marry whomever they please. But I also understand the anger of the women in *Jungle Fever*. In the movie, as in real life, the black women wind up celebrating each other. They know that, coming from each other, their expressions of support are more than just lip service.

Men Who Love to Stay

MARCH 14, 1990

The tipoff on my ex-friend Thomas came when I asked him for his home phone number.

"Well, uh," he stuttered. "I don't have a phone right now because of my situation . . ."

Thomas and I had been dating only a few weeks, but every

time I asked for his home number he hedged. He offered his beeper number and his number at work. I already had called his work number and he was never there. Beeping somebody isn't my style.

His situation, as he explained it, was that he didn't have an apartment of his own. He was temporarily staying with a friend, and there was no phone there he could use. That was his story.

I've known Thomas for eight years. He is not down and out. He has a Ph.D. in political science and a teaching job at a local college. He even has a car. But in all the time I've known him, he has never had a place of his own.

Over the few months we dated I learned that he has always lived around, sharing apartments with men friends or with whatever woman he was dating at the time. He was even married for a while. The lure of his fiancée's co-op must have been what tantalized him. When his short marriage failed, he went out on the circuit again.

During our brief relationship, the questions he asked me indicated he was apartment-shopping again—for my place. He took a keen interest in my redecorating efforts. A friend of his was selling a used leather sofa—cheap, he said. Why didn't I buy it? When I brought home a room divider for my living room he said he thought it would break up the apartment rather nicely in the event there were ever two people living there. *Hmmmmmmmm,* I thought.

After a few months I sent Thomas on his way, telling him he needed to look further for a new home. But he is an example of what my single women friends assure me is a growing phenomenon: homeless men. Oh, not the kind you see sleeping in the subways or working the streets in tattered clothes, their paper cups extended for a handout. These are able-bodied working men, often highly educated and employed as professionals. What they share is that they are social nomads, men who refuse to get a place of their own.

"I'm running into this roommate deal more and more, and I don't understand it," says my friend Valerie, who lives in Atlanta.

Her most recent male companion, John, a security guard

who's 40, at least has an apartment, but always needs room-mates to share the bills. He just lost one but immediately found another. "It's kind of pathetic," she said, stressing that the upshot of this situation is that he always comes over to her house.

I know a lot of women who are struggling. I don't have any women friends who are in their 30s or 40s who have room-mates. Many of us are underpaid, and yet we're paying out whatever it takes to keep our own places. In Atlanta you can still get an apartment for $300. I don't understand a man's not being able to get it together here.

It's a story I've heard over and over again—of couples who have played out the entire course of their relationships in the woman's house or apartment because the man has no place to call his own. They crash at our places, eat our food, watch movies on our VCRs, and never reciprocate with an invitation to be entertained in their homes. The men I'm talking about are earning from $12,000 to $80,000 a year. So this is apparently not so much an economic problem as it is a widespread malaise.

Listen to Tina's story. Tina is a law professor in her late 30s, a woman with a good job, an apartment, and some stability in her life. Not true of the men she's been meeting. "When I look back on the three men I've dated in the last seven years, there wasn't a lease among them," Tina says. "One lived with a friend. One was subletting an apartment. The other was living with his mother."

Then along came Kurt. Kurt was in his late 40s, brilliant, a professor at a prestigious law school, a man who earns royalties from a textbook he wrote. After he left his wife of 10 years, Kurt lived with several women before he met Tina. Then they started dating and he moved in with her. "The day he moved in he showed up at my door with his clothes in two Hefty bags," Tina told me. "I thought, here's a man who earns $80,000 a year. You'd think he could at least buy himself a set of luggage!"

Tina's relationship with Kurt lasted about a year. Then he disappeared one day while she was at work, leaving her a note saying he didn't want to be a burden to her. When I last talked to Tina, she said Kurt had moved in with another woman—this one an heiress.

"I think women feel they have to be more responsible," is the way my friend Jackie explains why women seem more inclined to make homes for themselves while many men simply wander. A woman's need for the security of knowing she has a roof over her head and where her next meal is coming from is more important than it is for a man.

And men get away with stuff like that more easily. How many men do you know who will take you in when you have nowhere to go and put up with you indefinitely?

Jackie tells the story of her cousin, 46, a schoolteacher who has signed one lease in his entire life, and signed that one when he got married. Ever since his divorce, which took place years ago, he has moved around; he now stays a while with buddies, a while with girlfriends—or goes back home to his mother.

Jackie also tells about her friend from the Midwest who came to New York to discuss a business venture and asked to stay at her apartment for two days. He wound up staying a month. "I had to feed him, and in the end I had to borrow money so he could get back home. What's more, he was a junk-food addict. After he left, I found Twinkies, bags of chips and all kinds of food hidden in the sofa, in dresser drawers, everywhere!"

The homeless-men problem appears to be a national one. Besides Tina in New York and Valerie in Atlanta, my friend Gilda in Detroit also has spotted it. She told me the story of a woman friend of hers, a fellow nurse with a good income and a house of her own. To her dismay, this friend is dating, and considering marrying, a man who lives at home with his mother.

It makes her angry, Gilda says. "She has all these assets to bring to a relationship. He has nothing. I tell her, look, he's living with his Mom because that's where he wants to be."

So what's to be said about this? Just that the problem of homelessness is far more pervasive than most people realize. It affects not just the unemployed, the down and out and the truly needy. It also affects the lazy, the unmotivated and the cheap—those who prefer living off someone else to putting down roots of their own.

So my single women friends and I have made a vow for the

1990s. The men we become involved with must have, at the very least, a lease and a phone number. We have hardened our hearts against the homeless. And not a minute too soon.

Kids Aren't What We Used to Be
DECEMBER 6, 1993

After the doorbell rang for the third time, she finally hobbled to the door. She must be in her 80s now, and her tiny body is doubled over from arthritis.

More than 30 years have passed since Martha McMillan was my sixth-grade teacher, but pain has not dulled the sharpness of her mind.

On this visit we talked of many things. She asked if I had been following the news stories about the anniversary of President Kennedy's assassination. Then she explained to me in detail that it wasn't Lee Harvey Oswald who shot Kennedy, but a hitman hired by the CIA because they were angered by Kennedy's performance during the Bay of Pigs. She showed me a well-worn paperback book that expounds this theory.

As we've done on my previous visits to my hometown of Birmingham, Ala., we talked about her travels after illness forced her to retire from teaching. Physical pain didn't keep her from visiting more countries than most of us will ever see, and she recalled the beauty of Israel and the squalor of parts of India.

We talked about school. "When you were just a little girl, your brother was in my class," she said. "I guess he must have told you about me, because one day you brought me a note that said, 'You are my favorite teacher.'" She seemed to take a lot of satisfaction from this.

I remember her as a tough, but kind teacher, with a sense of humor and a laugh that started with a cackle and ended with her bent over and breathless with laughter. She had a low tolerance for nonsense, and was known to tell a rowdy student that if she didn't stop clowning, she'd throw a book at his head.

Math was her subject and she taught it with great relish.

She would call two students at a time to the blackboard, give us a problem to solve, and we'd race to see who could get the answer first. The winner got to take on the next challenger.

Mrs. McMillan was a teacher who looked life in the eye, and that realism came across to me. "Poor girls," she once said, giving me my first taste of feminism. "Boys grow up being treated like they're so special and entitled to everything, and meanwhile girls have to do all the work!"

She taught us Spanish, and the few phrases I know in that language I learned from her. And she read us poetry—serious poems about life and death, some verses I can still recite today.

She wanted us to succeed, got agitated when we messed up, and knew us well. She never forgot the score I made on the national reading exam when I was in her class. You scored 13.1—the same level as a freshman in college!

Those of us who were her students were lucky to have her. In the 1950s and '60s, Birmingham, Ala., was a grim place where even smart and well-mannered black children were treated badly when they ventured outside their own neighborhoods. Alabama vied with Mississippi for having the worst schools in the nation—and those were the white schools. The state spent one-half as much on black schools.

But miracles happened in those schools because there was a constellation of teachers like Mrs. McMillan. There was Mrs. Mosely, my kind first-grade teacher, who showed up at my parents' house 20 years later to bring me a wedding gift. There was soft-spoken Mrs. Southall, who led my Brownie troop while working hard to send her son to medical school. Mrs. Terrill exposed us to art and made fabulous sets for school variety shows. And brilliant Mr. Shepard helped us with our science projects and took us on trips.

In high school, Mrs. Veale and Mrs. Martin taught math with the reverence usually reserved for religion, while Mr. Stokes taught us to dream of big jobs, big degrees and big lives. Mrs. Thornton, all energy, personality and drive, taught us to love everything French, while Ms. Woolfolk, who taught us about politics, had a vision that reached far beyond the segregated boundaries of Birmingham.

Even within this grim version of American apartheid, they

and our parents created a world for us that was normal, nurturing and rich.

"Kids just aren't like they used to be," Mrs. Thornton, who is now retired, told me recently. "They're not interested in anything, and they don't want to learn anything. So many of our children are in trouble, even our middle-class children.

"Of course, most of us came from homes with two parents. We weren't into sex, teenage pregnancy was rare and considered scandalous and drugs were almost unheard of. Most of us never even saw a gun."

Last week the New York City Board of Education revealed that last year it confiscated almost 300 guns, knives and other weapons from pre-high-school age children alone—that's the current reality of life in the schools.

There are still teachers like Mrs. McMillan and the others I knew as a child, who are trying to help children grow up right. There are still children who, while living in less than ideal circumstances, are grasping what their teachers have to offer.

But visiting my old teachers made me realize how lucky we were and how many barriers now separate too many children from the magic we knew.

Buying a Co-op, Taxing Nerves
FEBRUARY 14, 1990

At 4 A.M. the other day I was jolted out of my sleep by what felt like a slap on the head. I crawled to the foot of my bed and turned on the TV set. Would I spend another morning watching Ben Casey reruns and grade-B movies?

I stared at the screen and waited for the by-now-familiar symptoms to subside: the restlessness, the fluttering in my chest, the cold stab of fear. I knew this was not an attack of mere insomnia, or even anxiety over my next column. This was a case of Apartment Buyer's Panic.

I've suffered from this terrible disease for the last month, ever since I decided to buy a co-op, a decision I once swore I'd never make. It is a painful illness, but one I am told I will learn to live with in time, provided I get lots of love and support from my friends and a big raise from my boss. How did it ever come to this?

Eight years ago, when my friends started buying their apartments, I couldn't understand why. Susan, a newspaper reporter, scraped together the $5,000 down payment to buy her $30,000 studio. It was a bland, one-room affair in the West Village, and she justified the purchase by saying it was a good investment. It beat renting, she said, which gave you no tax break, and if one was planning to stay in New York, what else was there to do?

I was no more convinced when Julie, my former boss's secretary, bought her East Side studio for about the same price. For both, raising the down payment was a struggle, but they seemed to view the act of buying an apartment as grabbing a stake in the future. To me, it just didn't seem worth it.

You see, I am from the South, and I grew up believing the only home worth buying was a house with a yard. Buying a condo or a co-op was an illusion. You paid lots of money and went into debt, only to own the same few rooms you already lived in. Only now you were poorer and couldn't afford to go anywhere, so you spent all your time shut up in those same meager rooms.

A co-op was even worse than a condo because you didn't even own the rooms, only a share in a corporation that owned the rooms. Both devices were schemes that allowed greedy landlords to earn hundreds of thousands of extra dollars by selling off bits and pieces of the buildings they were renting out. The only scam worse than this, I thought, was a time-share, where you bought a few rooms, but only got to use them one or two weeks a year.

Now I am on the verge of buying my own co-op. I have applied for a bank mortgage and am waiting to hear if I'm accepted by the bank. I can also look forward to my grilling at the hands of the co-op board, a process some of my apartment-owning friends compare to being worked over by cops in a bare, brightly lit room. I have described the process I am going through to my friends, and they counsel me, each in his or her own way. Here are some of their responses:

"That's exciting!" gushed my friend Gail, who lives in Boston and has never owned a piece of real estate in her life. "It may not seem like much to you, but it's exciting to me."

"If I had the money to buy a place, I'd buy one," said my friend Carla, who has never known the joy of writing a check for more than $12,000.

"You're stealing this apartment!" my real estate agent said in a hushed voice, referring to the relatively low purchase price. I remained quiet, thinking that the only thing being stolen was my money.

"You must be crazy!" said my friend Jesse. "You'll spend all that money and all you're going to own is a pile of bricks!"

What is it that really bothers me most about buying my own apartment?

The money, to begin with. I wince at the thought of tripling my monthly housing costs, of the new furniture I must buy, the repairs I will have to make. It's also the idea of looting my savings, which I have watched grow over the years with the pleasure of a kid filling a piggy-bank. And there's the prospect of not having as much spending money.

I've been a person who hasn't had to agonize about buying new clothes, taking a vacation or renting a car. Now I figure I'll have to stick to a strict allowance. (One friend of mine, a real estate writer who's trading in her studio-sized co-op for a one-bedroom, claims she was so poor after she bought her first place that she ate popcorn for days afterward.) When the fear gets out of control, I have nightmares of being unable to make the mortgage payments, of slipping down, down, down into that cycle of poverty and despair we reporters are always writing about.

"Excuse me," I see myself saying to people on the subway, as I dangle a cardboard cup. "I am not a dope addict, and I'm not out here robbing or killing anybody. But I do have a mortgage payment to make. Anything you can give would be appreciated."

I must admit that part of what bothers me about apartment ownership is also the idea of feeling tied down, of no longer having the flexibility to make quick changes on impulse—to move to another city if I feel so inclined.

So why am I buying this co-op, you ask? First, I've gotten to that stage where I feel that to be an adult one should own something. It's partly that I may equate making a change with making progress, may feel I'm not successful if I'm not visibly moving upward. Finally, I'm buying the apartment because I like it. It is pretty and it has the amenities I have always dreamed of: the doorman, the polished wood walls in the elevator, the stained glass windows in the lobby, the hardwood floors. Just walking into the building lifts my spirits, and these days one can use every boost one gets.

Still, in the wee hours of the morning, terrible thoughts fill my mind: I'm getting into the real estate market at the very time that the market is crashing. I tell myself that when I sell the apartment I may lose money. My friends may have bought studios for $30,000 and sold them for $125,000, but things will never be that good again.

As I agonize over my decision in the morning hours, sometimes I am visited by a gentle spirit who appears on my TV screen. He is a round, elderly man, and he walks toward me pushing a shopping cart. In one hand he holds a box of oatmeal. He moves closer and I recognize his face. It is Wilford Brimley. He looks into my eyes and, like a kind angel, utters the words I need to hear.

He says: "It's the right thing to do."

A Christmas Essay
DECEMBER 24, 1991

It was the Christmas of my ninth or 10th year. I don't remember exactly, except that it was the Christmas I got Cindy, my bride doll.

She was waiting there under the tree when I emerged from my bedroom on Christmas morning, wide awake after a feverish night of insomnia brought on by my anticipation of Christmas Day. She wore a white satin dress trimmed in lace, and a veil trailed from her bobbed hair. She had red lips, dark brown eyes and a face that was pretty yet seemed more intelligent than those of most other dolls. She was black, too, a deep brown color, the richness of which still surprises me when I look at her now.

As with all the Christmases that preceded this one, Cindy was the most highly prized of my new toys, the cherished doll. And it was her arrival that prompted my mother to exclaim: "Oh, let's have a wedding!"

You must understand the special place that dolls occupied in my growing up. Since as far back as I can remember, I always got a new doll for Christmas. And that doll became for me the centerpiece of the day. The very first one was Yvette, who arrived when I was a year old. I don't remember that Christmas at all, or getting the doll, but I have Yvette to this day. She sits on top of a bookshelf in my old bedroom in my parents' house. She wears her original blue satin dress trimmed with ruffles. The material is delicate, worn thin by washings over the years. She wears a matching bonnet over black hair that has lost most of its curl. Her lips are red and two real teeth are in her slightly opened mouth. The teeth are somewhat recessed, having been knocked back from years of handling. Like Cindy, Yvette is also black, one of the few black dolls in my collection. When I was growing up, in the '50s and '60s, there weren't very many black dolls, so she and Cindy are unique. Yvette is also special, because she is my oldest doll and the one that bears my middle name.

I have always been fascinated with dolls. I get this from my mother, who, I suppose, may have longed for fancy dolls when she was growing up during the Depression. I know choosing a new doll for me each Christmas seemed to delight her as much as getting them did me. I don't remember the names of most of my dolls, and there were so many of them that even their faces are a blur. I know there was the three-foot high walking doll with the long blonde hair; a very French-looking doll with porcelain skin that wore a stylish dress and an upswept hairdo; and there were Barbie and Ken and their pals, including a fluffy pet poodle. Barbie and the others were my last dolls, acquired when I was 13 and starting to be too old for such childish amusements.

Until then, however, each Christmas I carried my new doll around with me to the homes of my girlfriends. They showed me their toys, and I showed off my latest doll. I took very good care of my doll children. Some girls are obsessed with combing and brushing their dolls' hair, which means that a month after Christmas their poor dolls are half bald and missing their underpants, a shoe or sock and a few buttons from the harsh treatment to which their owners had subjected them. But my dolls never looked like orphans. Not wanting to disrupt their carefully set hairstyles, I refrained from combing my dolls' hair. I also knew that dust was an enemy of dolls' hair. If it accumulated, it made the synthetic hair dry and dull. I remember blowing the dust off my dolls' heads regularly, and as a result even these many years later their hair retains most of the original gloss and shape. Nor did any of my dolls get thrown away. I still have 20 or so of them, and they look pretty much the same as when I was a kid. Most of them sit around my old bedroom, while others are packed away in closets.

Once, when I returned home from college, I noticed that a couple of my dolls looked a little beat-up. It seems my grandmother had allowed the little girl next door to play with them in my absence, and the child had not treated the dolls well. I was not pleased. I believe dolls should be handled gently, like delicate children.

Anyway, that particular Christmas my mother came up with the idea of having a doll wedding. As she described her vision of it, I became as excited as she. We'd hold a wedding ceremony and have Cindy married properly, and we'd invite all my girlfriends to the event. Once the idea was hatched, plans for the wedding proceeded at a feverish pace. The first obstacle was to find Cindy a suitable groom. I owned no boy dolls, and the closest thing I had to one was a Howdy Doody hand puppet. The problem was, being a hand puppet, Howdy had no legs. I guess you could say it was like taking a man with rough edges but plenty of potential and molding him into husband material. Using stuff we had around the house—maybe it was some empty paper towel rolls—my mother fashioned some legs for Howdy and dressed him in a little tuxedo she had sewn. When we got through with him, the red-haired, freckled Mr. Doody cut a dashing figure as the groom.

There were dresses to be made for the bridesmaids, which

were chosen from among my stable of dolls. My mother sewed these dresses herself, and I believe there were three or four bridesmaids. Invitations went out to my cadre of girlfriends. On the appointed day, the wedding took place in the den of our house. With my friends sitting around in their dressy dresses, wearing braids and ribbons or with their hair done up in holiday curls, they sat around the den, waiting for the wedding to begin.

It started with my mother's playing "Here Comes the Bride" on the piano. I marched the dolls into the room—first the bridesmaids, then Howdy Doody in his tuxedo and finally Cindy, who was a radiant and serene bride. I can't recall who conducted the marriage ceremony, but I know that in my role as the mother of the bride, who was losing a daughter (and gaining only a hand puppet for a son-in-law), I sobbed loudly throughout the ceremony. Afterwards I collected myself, and my friends and I feasted on cake and other goodies my mother had prepared for the reception.

In the panoply of events that made up my childhood, the doll wedding stands out as one of the most magical. To begin with, it was fun. It was a chance to put on a show, to act out an adult spectacle on a small scale. Second, and immensely important for a pre-adolescent, it impressed my friends, who had never seen such a thing and who would never have thought of putting on a doll wedding of their own.

In later years my friends would tell me that they thought I came from the perfect family, that my parents were the kind of parents they always wished they'd had. I'm sure their fantasies about us were fueled by events like the doll wedding, which must have seemed wonderfully inventive to them. The fact was my parents were not perfect, and my childhood was riddled with as much pain as any other. But I now understand how the impact of this mini-spectacle on their girlish minds could have made them regard my family differently.

Finally, the doll wedding revealed my mother's imagination, her sense of fun and childishness, which sometimes got lost amid the responsibilities of working as a schoolteacher and taking care of a household that included her husband, two children and her mother.

You might say it was the power of her imagination that

infused much of my childhood. Its spark was always there, and it created magic for me in other ways than just a doll's wedding at Christmas. Not just her love of dolls, but also her love of books, which I inherited, and her love of music. She was a music teacher and insisted that I start piano lessons when I was 7. I studied piano for nine years and eventually abandoned it, to her bitter disappointment. But that exposure gave me a love of music that continues to this day. My piano-playing has long since been upstaged by singing. But I do have a piano of my own, a gift from my parents. And if I had a daughter, I think I would give her a doll wedding and play the wedding march for her, too.

It is ironic the doll wedding took place in front of a grim backdrop of racial oppression that suffused my hometown of Birmingham, Ala., like a noxious vapor. As black people, we were amazingly limited by law and custom. There were so many places we couldn't go—to the downtown public library, the public parks and swimming pools, restaurants, the movie theaters, except for two black theaters and the balcony of a white one. There were so many things we couldn't do. In all of Birmingham there were three restaurants blacks could frequent: a coffee house owned by the local black millionaire and a couple of barbecue joints. A treat for my brother and me was to get my father to drive us to the black Dairy Queen way across town.

Yet, in the midst of this stifling atmosphere, our parents managed to create an existence for us that seemed normal. I took dance lessons, piano lessons. My family traveled north to Chicago, Detroit, New York, Washington to visit friends and relatives. There was the church, which offered ordinary people a place to shine and exert power they had no place else in the world. And there were events like the doll wedding.

Years later, after I had gone north to college and worked for a while in the Northeast, I stopped going home for Christmas. For a decade I didn't spend a single Christmas in the South. There were many reasons. Tensions within my family. The constant drain of their expectations of me. The feeling that I no longer belonged in the South, that it was a foreign country with small-minded people. Instead, like my other younger colleagues at whatever news outfit I was working at the time, I volunteered to work each Christmas Day.

But eventually the solitude of spending Christmas away from family and in the company of other holiday orphans grew wearing. I wanted to be at home for Christmas, and the city, even with all its excitement and possibilities, no longer felt like home. So I started going south again.

This year I will spend Christmas with my family in Jacksonville, Fla., where my brother lives with his family and where my parents will come to spend Christmas Day. My niece, now 15, loves dolls, too. She owns a whole orphanage of Cabbage Patch Kids and a large contingent of Barbies. As she's grown up, I have contributed to her doll collection, taking as much pride in her growing family as my mother once did in mine. My niece takes good care of her dolls, too, just as I did. But in a few years she will leave home for college and leave her dolls behind.

One day she, too, may want to put distance between herself and her family, and probably, in time, she will want to come back. I don't know what childhood memories will draw her back, but I hope they are as vivid and magical for her as the memory of my doll's wedding is for me. Then both of us will have come full circle.

This Customer's V-A-R-I Hot Over Collar

SEPTEMBER 19, 1994

I know I ought to be writing about Jimmy Carter's trip to Haiti or the latest DNA evidence in the O.J. Simpson case. But I can't. I'm too filled with rage toward a New York City store called Vari Zioni.

That's V-A-R-I Z-I-O-N-I. Remember that name. After last week, I will never shop there again.

Vari Zioni is a chain of smart women's clothing stores scattered around Manhattan. They sell stylish creations from all over the world, and I have bought several outfits there. But listen to this story:

A month ago, I got married. For my nuptial costume, I picked an outfit from Vari Zioni. After I went to several other stores and tried on various flimsy, flowing dresses that made me look like Roseanne, a helpful saleswoman at Vari Zioni showed me a three-piece outfit that was just right. It consisted of a long, chiffon-like skirt of cream-colored silk, a matching vest and a black silk blazer with cream-colored collar and lapels.

"That's much more becoming," she told me, while another saleswoman gushed from the sidelines. When I paid for my outfit, the store manager, who also operated the cash register, told me what a wonderful outfit I was getting, and that he hoped I would enjoy it.

I wore the outfit for my wedding and a few weeks later for our reception. Several people said they thought it was elegant and one friend told me it looked very Streisand. I was thrilled because, since it wasn't some frilly, bridal-looking thing, I knew I'd be able to wear it again.

Last week I took it to be dry cleaned. But the next day the cleaner called to say they had tested the jacket. Because of the make-up of dyes in the jacket, they told me, it couldn't be cleaned without the black dye running like a river onto the cream-colored collar and lapels. I told them I'd come and pick it up.

I took it back to Vari Zioni and explained the problem to the manager who rang up the sale a month earlier. He had been extremely solicitous when I paid him $600 for the three pieces a month before, but now as I told him my story, he barely glanced at the jacket and shrugged his shoulders.

"You should take it to a good cleaner," he told me.

"My cleaner is a good cleaner. I've been using them for years," I said.

"Well, that outfit was made by a very reputable company and I know they wouldn't have made it without testing it first to see if it would run."

I asked him if he'd like to send it to a cleaner of the store's choice, if he didn't believe mine.

"No, I'm not going to send it to the cleaner," he said.

Meanwhile, the only saleswoman in the store listened, but

said nothing, her eyes avoiding mine. It's funny how the same people who are so eager to help when you're buying something turn lethargic or downright hostile when faced with the possibility of having to give you a refund.

Finally, the manager spit out the name of a cleaner a couple of blocks away. "That's a good cleaner," he said. "Take it there."

I walked up the street to the cleaner he recommended and explained my problem. The manager said he would test the jacket and get back to me.

He called me last Friday to tell me the grim news: "This jacket cannot be cleaned without the black dye running onto the white," he said. "It can't be cleaned without running the chance of ruining it."

I took a cab down to the cleaners, got the jacket and returned to Vari Zioni.

"I'm back," I said. "I took this to the cleaner you recommended and they say they can't clean it either." I handed him a note from that cleaner and from my own, saying as much.

"Well, take it to another cleaner," he said.

"I'm not going to run around to every cleaner in New York," I said. Again, I asked if he wanted to send it to a cleaner of his choice.

"I'm not going to send it anywhere," he said. "We've sold twenty or thirty of these jackets and we've never had a complaint," he told me.

"Well, I'm certainly having a problem with mine," I said. "Plus, I spent three hundred dollars on this jacket."

"Three hundred dollars is not a lot of money," he said. "People spend more money on clothes than that."

"It might not be much money to you," I said. "But three hundred dollars is a lot of money to me. You know, there is a difference between a good store and a bad store. When you buy something at Saks and you have a problem, they fix it, or give you another item or give you your money back."

"You ought to shop at Saks, then!" he told me.

He eyed my jacket suspiciously. "Why do you want to get it cleaned, anyway? The jacket is clean."

I pointed to the dirt ring around the collar. "What good is a jacket that I can't ever have cleaned?" I asked. Finally, he told me he wasn't going to listen to me anymore. He flung the jacket on the counter.

"I'm not going to listen to any more of this. Leave my store!" he ordered.

I didn't budge. I was the only customer in the store, so he had no one else to turn his attention to, and I guess he realized I wasn't going anywhere.

Finally he said roughly: "All right, leave the jacket," and he wrote up a claim check for me.

"What are you going to do with it?" I asked.

He said he would try to find a cleaner that would do it. He told me to come back in a week.

I left the store and took a cab to work, feeling angry and badly abused. At my office, I called another Vari Zioni store and asked if there was a store headquarters where I could complain about the manager at the Broadway store. The man said there was no headquarters, but that he'd look into it.

I called the New York City Department of Consumer Affairs, described the encounter and asked for a complaint form, which I plan to file with them.

I now have two-thirds of an outfit that cost me $600, and which I had hoped to wear for years to come. I am mad as hell.

So, no, I am not writing about world events today. Most of us don't understand what they mean, anyway. Everybody can understand what I'm talking about.

Look Around
JANUARY 24, 1994

Now that Lorena Bobbitt has gotten off, perhaps the jokes that surrounded her and John will subside.

The jury accepted the theory that John's abuse caused Lorena to snap, and has sent her off to a mental ward, instead of to jail.

But the ridicule with which we regard the Bobbitts lingers. We look at their messy lives and low-class behavior with disdain and agree with the journalist who described them as the couple from Wal-Mart. Their lives are like a bad comedy, and we feel superior. We'd never behave like the Bobbitts—this shiftless dummy and his wife, the ditz.

But in reality the Bobbitts are far from unique. All the research on domestic violence shows that the Bobbitt scenario is a common one. By one estimate, one in two women are battered by boyfriends or husbands at some point in their lives, and an estimated three million women are currently victims of domestic violence.

Nor are they all lower-middle class trash like the Bobbitts. The violence crosses all economic levels, all kinds of neighborhoods, and the stories are wild and crazy, the parties just as scattered as John and Lorena. If you want to know what a wife-beater or a battered wife looks like, just look at the man or woman sitting next to you. Just ask the other woman.

When Lorena testified about the beatings that started one month after she married John, the other woman remembered that hers started a month after she got married. John assaulted Lorena when she asked him to turn down the TV. The other woman's husband went into a rage when she ate the remains of some Jell-O in the refrigerator. For this she was shouted at, punched and thrown around the room.

When Lorena told about the fight she and John had at the beach when men whistled at her and John hit her and they left the beach early, the other woman remembered the time at the beach when her husband went swimming and another couple offered her a piece of fried chicken. When her husband found out he went into a rage and called her ugly names. She picked up a rock and threatened to hit him. They left the beach early, too.

When Lorena told of John's verbal abuse, including showing her a list of women who were willing to sleep with him since Lorena wasn't woman enough, the other woman remembered her husband's telling her there was no point in leaving him because no one else would want her anyway. Her husband also had a list—of wifely duties that grew longer every day.

Lorena told about the time John refused to let her drive the car because he didn't trust her with a stick-shift. He backed up the car and knocked her down with the car door, she said. The other woman remembered the times her husband refused to let her drive her own car because, according to him, it never drove right after she'd been at the wheel.

When Lorena testified to standing in the kitchen after John raped her and had flashbacks of the beatings, the rapes, the forced abortion and the verbal assaults, the other woman remembered the flashbacks she'd had of the time her husband threw her down, and sat on top of her while banging her head against the floor.

Lorena Bobbitt grabbed a knife from the kitchen and cut John. The other woman once slept with a knife under her pillow to fend off an attack. She never used the knife, but while riding the subway she would have visions of stabbing him to death.

A recurring theme in the Lorena Bobbitt trial was that under the law fear and insanity are the only acceptable reasons for defending oneself with a weapon, while anger and revenge are not. But that is contrary to human nature and commonsense.

Assume that a man was held captive by another man, was abused and sodomized and then the abuser fell into a drunken sleep. When he was able to, we'd expect the abused guy to get up and kill his tormentor, perhaps mutilating him later. We would applaud it as a reasonable response to the intolerable insult he had suffered.

Yet many of us expected Lorena to collect herself, get dressed, walk to a phone, and call the police. Even in abuse, we expect women to act civilized and ladylike.

Now the jury has acquitted Lorena Bobbitt, and while not advocating that other women do what she did, I think they were right.

I am that other woman, and while I didn't cut or mutilate anyone, I feel no superiority to Lorena. The difference in our outcomes I attribute to luck, or some presence or mind, or a click in the head that came soon enough for me, but too late for her.

Any of us who smugly look down on this Wal-Mart couple are no better than the Bobbitts. Plenty of us live, or have lived, in the five-and-dime.

Chapter 2

Women and men

A Poolside Version of Date Rape?

JULY 7, 1993

Dripping wet in her fuchsia swimsuit, her long legs dangling into the pool, Nakima Wilson explained to me the adolescent ritual of dunking.

"The boys dunk us when we're inside the pool," said Nakima, who is 15. "They pick you up and throw you up in the air and you fall back down in the water. I like it. It's fun."

But Serene Thomas, who is 10 and therefore has an entirely different perspective on such things, disagreed.

"I don't like it," she said. "They throw you up too far and when you hit the water it hurts."

Somewhere in the gap between Nakima's thinking and Serene's—well, therein lay the rub, as regulars at the Crotona Park swimming pool in the Bronx puzzled over the stripping and traumatizing of a 14-year-old girl swimmer this week.

Anybody you talked to at the pool yesterday, adult or child, could tell you about dunking. It's an adolescent mating game, really. The kids' hormones are perking, and adolescence is a time when boys are so mute around girls they can attract attention only through physical bravado. They may tussle with each other, swat the girls, or tug at their clothes. In the pool, they pick up the girls and throw them into the water.

Wanda Pubill, her 6-year-old daughter in tow, said she'd never allow her little girl into the pool unaccompanied if she were 13. "The guys get rough with the girls. Some of the girls like it, but some of them don't, and that's what the problem is."

Troy Johnson, 15, who sat on a concrete bleacher nearby, was the personification of Pubill's worst fears.

"The girls be likin' it," Johnson said when I asked him if he dunked. "You throw them up in the air and they like it. They tell us they like it."

I asked Troy what he got out of dunking. "We do it so we can feel on their titties . . . They like us pulling on their titties. You get a lot out of it later on, you know?"

I asked him if he meant that dunking was a prelude to sex.

He nodded and said that horseplay in the pool made some girls give it up faster.

Chris Santiago, at 20 one of the older guys around the pool, said this version of dunking was a tradition he endorsed. "Yeah, touching and feeling girls' breasts and butts, and if they tell me they don't like it, I'll stop. There are other girls in there who will like it. Then, later, we go in the back and get busy." He extended his arms and gestured toward the expansive grounds of Crotona Park.

The problem with boys in search of girls who'll go in the back is that sometimes they pick the wrong girls. Then you have a clash between those who see dunking as innocent horseplay and those who view it as foreplay. The result can be a poolside version of date rape, except that the participants are adolescents, not adults, and the setting is not a frat house or a basement, but a public park.

On the day that a 14-year-old girl who only wanted to swim was frightened to the point of terror, 16-year-old Terrence Brown was in the pool. "The guards didn't have no control of the pool," Terrence said. "It was like 30 guys with one leader. They were going around screaming and chanting, 'Whoot, there it is!' They'd grab the girls by the legs—'one, two, three,' in the water. They be holding to their bathing suits and ripping.

"They were all in a bunch doing it to girls they didn't know. It got out of hand. I heard screaming. And I saw the girl come up. Her bra popped."

I asked Terrence how the girl looked and he seemed embarrassed to tell me exactly what he saw. "I just looked, and said, 'Hey, that's wrong.'"

Yesterday folks at the pool were blaming the city for lax security and saying the incident never would have happened if there had been some cops and more lifeguards at the pool on Monday. On Tuesday I counted nine lifeguards, four cops and a handful of Parks Department attendants. Parks Commissioner Betsy Gotbaum even showed up and promised to have police stationed at every city pool during open hours.

But it only takes a second or two for a mating ritual to evolve from play to abuse. No cop can move that fast. Only the values police can control a situation like that.

Much Ado about Maples

DECEMBER 15, 1993

"Which one is she?" the elderly man asked, pushing from behind me to a position which totally blocked my view.

"She's the one with the long blonde hair," said somebody in the crowd, as if there were somebody in New York City who doesn't know what Marla Maples looks like. Maybe the guy was from Cedar Rapids.

"She's beautiful, isn't she," cooed the woman next to me, but I was craning my neck, trying to see Marla, so I didn't answer.

This was what it was like at Macy's yesterday, as Marla swept into a mob of Christmas shoppers to show off her new line of maternity clothes. Marla, who is planning her wedding next week to Donald Trump, floated in—flanked by an entourage that included four impossibly thin models, each done up in an evening outfit and wearing lots of glittering jewelry. They were so thin they made a mockery of the way a typical woman looks when she's pregnant.

"Are you really pregnant?" I asked one of them, who was wearing a filmy little black number and whose stomach was only slightly round.

"It's just a little padding," she said, rubbing it lovingly with her hand.

Several hundred people had gathered on the seventh floor of Macy's to see Marla, having fought their way through racks of chenille sweaters and displays of Lamb Chop puppets to see a woman whose maternity collection made it to the racks two weeks before she got to show off her wedding dress.

"Marla! Marla!" the photographers shouted, trying to get her attention and a good shot of her face.

"Marla! Marla!" a TV reporter shouted, trying to lure her over for an interview.

I must admit that Marla looked wonderful and acted very graciously toward her fans. Perhaps motherhood (daughter Tiffany was born in October) and finally treeing the elusive Donald have mellowed her out. In the past, she has been known to throw fits in public.

"I want to thank all of you for coming," she beamed. "It's really been a good week for me personally."

She told the crowd she had decided to help design a collection of maternity clothes because her own pregnancy had given her the greatest experience of all—the gift of life!

Marla's Maternity Moods line is for the woman who refuses to let a 30-pound weight gain or swollen legs ruin her social life. The collection is made up completely of party clothes, which seems appropriate coming from the current grand dame of the Taj Mahal casino. In price, though, the clothes are more Ramada Inn than Trump Plaza.

There's a white chiffon number with a lacy blouse that has faux-pearl buttons, and a matching skirt and jacket, $98. The black chiffon ensemble with double-breasted jacket and see-through long sleeves also sells for $98. There's a green satin dress with off-the-shoulder bodice that goes for $164. And for the expectant mother who still wants to play Batwoman, there are the black leggings with a matching blouse, flared at the waist.

"It's exciting, very exciting," said Jackie Terry Gantzer of the clothes she designed for Marla. Designers love to use the word exciting.

"The line does stand alone," Macy's buyer Lynne Papa said. "It's more fashionable than some of our other maternity lines."

I approached three saleswomen in the maternity section to ask how the Marla line has been selling since it hit the store a week ago, but they gave me blank stares and remained mute. I figured they were over-excited like everyone else.

After posing with the models, Marla sat down and autographed 8×10 glossy photographs of herself for her fans, none of whom appeared to be pregnant.

When I asked Keiko Reitz of Brooklyn if she was expecting, she said no, she just wanted to see what Marla Maples looked like in person. "I'm 54 and if I had a child now I'd be in Ripley's Believe It Or Not!"

Of Marla, Reitz said, "She's really quite lovely and she seems very nice."

"I came to see how many lines are in her face," said Mary

Ondrejka, who works in advertising for Macy's. "She has lines in her face. She looks her age."

Rosemary Flynn of Long Island had brought her 9-year-old daughter, Kiera, to see Santa Claus, and was attracted by all the commotion. Little Kiera said she thought Marla was nice, but when I asked if she was more excited about seeing Santa Claus or Donald Trump's fiancée, she deadpanned: "I really wasn't excited about either one."

We are fascinated with people like Marla because they prove that the rich, the beautiful and the well-connected can be as tacky in their personal lives as the rest of us—although, unlike us, they have no good excuse.

One shopper, who wouldn't give me her name, said she had previously met Donald, Ivana and Marla, and considered them trash.

"It's just a shame that people who have money don't have more taste, especially since they're up in our faces all the time," she sneered.

Even calling their daughter Tiffany. "Aren't names like Tiffany and Jennifer out of fashion?"

But as Marla sets off on what could well be a bumpy ride with Donald, not even the flintiest heart could help wishing her well.

"I'm sure she's nice," the shopper said.

We Haven't Heard the Real Story
NOVEMBER 7, 1994

"Susan seemed to be one of the best mothers in the world," Sara Singleton, the great-grandmother of Michael and Alexander Smith, said when she learned that the boys' own mother had confessed to killing them.

Like everyone else who followed this story about the murder of two innocent children, Singleton said she felt betrayed by Susan Smith's tale of a black abductor, and by her tearful public pleas for the return of her children. "I felt as if I had trusted her and she had let everybody down."

In the end, Susan Smith's little boys were destroyed by a lie. She was willing, it would appear, to murder her own children rather than admit to the world that she was not a perfect mother.

Beset by personal and financial problems, Smith had lost a husband and been dumped by a boyfriend who didn't want to be bothered with children. She could have given Michael, 3, and Alexander, 14 months, away, if all she wanted was to be rid of them. But it is hard to find an example of greater scorn than that which faces a mother who gives away her children.

Instead, Susan Smith apparently pushed them into the lake, lied about it, and hoped she wouldn't get caught. For a while she had exactly what she wanted. She was free of her children and she won the highest accolade the nation bestows on a woman—its sympathy for a bereaved mother.

The popular sentiment now says that a public stoning would be too good a punishment for Susan Smith. This is because a mother who would kill her own children flies in the face of the Mother Love Myth. This myth says that no love is greater than a mother's love for her child, and that a good mother would sacrifice anything, even to the point of killing or being killed, to protect her children.

However, reality tells us that while women commit far fewer crimes than men, the one crime category they dominate is the murder of their own children.

This is nothing new. In Greek mythology, Medea, the wife of Jason, killed her two children to get back at her husband for having an affair with another woman. She also poisoned the mistress. Then she went on to have a child by another man. Of course Medea was a truly evil woman who killed anyone who thwarted her ambitions.

In 1983, Diane Downs, a divorced postal worker in Oregon, shot her three kids so they wouldn't interfere with her relationship with her boyfriend. A sick and narcissistic woman, Downs loved having babies. She acted as a surrogate mother for a couple who couldn't have children, and she was pregnant again when she went on trial for shooting her own children.

In Britain, children under the age of 1 are four times more likely to be the victims of murder than any other age group. And if we didn't have so many young men shooting each other to death in the United States, child murder would be at the top of the crime list here.

Mothers don't like to admit it, but for many there have been times when they felt like killing their children, or at least wished their child gone, if not exactly dead.

At a time when marriage is crumbling, careers are being aborted in mid-life, and priests are revealed to be child molesters, the Mother Love Myth is all we have left.

So the people of Union, S.C., saw Susan Smith and her cute little boys and wrapped her in the myth of the perfect mother. Now they are angry because two children are dead and they feel she betrayed them.

The reality is that Susan Smith and her family were falling apart, and only in the weeks to come will we begin to hear the sorry details that were glossed over all along.

Scared Straight
MAY 30, 1994

This is the story of Grace and Harry, and how some insurance companies brought peace to their marriage.

It started one night in April 1993, when Harry came home late and found Grace in a bad mood. They'd been married for three years and had a young daughter, but lately things had been tense between them.

Grace, who worked for a phone company, had just changed jobs. They had recently moved and were now in the process of building a house. Harry's best friend and his father had died within a few months of each other. And Harry, a self-employed mason, had started going out by himself. They argued a lot.

This night, when Harry came home, he made some remark that made Grace mad.

"I'm really getting sick of you," she said. "I want to get away from you."

Harry's response was to go into the bedroom and knock all the items on the dressers onto the floor. Then he headed out the front door. That's when Grace slugged him. Harry grabbed her and slung her around, at which point Grace stumbled and fell onto a trunk, which gouged the side of her hip. It bruised up pretty badly.

She called the police and told them what happened, but they said if they came to her house they would arrest her as well as Harry, since she had hit him first. Worried about what would happen to their daughter if they both went to jail, Grace told the police not to come.

She left and went to stay at her mother's. The next day she saw a lawyer about getting an order of protection against Harry, and she went to a doctor because she wanted it on the record that Harry had hurt her.

"I had it documented," Grace said. "I wanted him to know that I'm not a punching bag and that this was serious and that it was never going to happen again. I also wanted him to realize that a divorce could be a real ugly scene."

Grace and Harry reconciled and agreed that in the future they wouldn't let their arguments get out of hand. Grace moved back in two days after she left.

Three months later, in July, she applied for some life insurance for the two of them. They wanted to switch companies because their premiums were too high. She applied to First Colonie, which wrote her a letter saying she'd been turned down. The letter didn't say why, but referred her to her medical records.

Then she applied to State Farm, which said it was refusing coverage because of domestic violence in her past. They had also seen her doctor's report about the incident with Harry. State Farm said Grace could reapply in another year.

"I was statistically a high risk because a woman in a domestic violence situation, they said it usually recurs. It was like a slap in the face. I was really upset."

Grace was afraid to tell Harry about this, even after their old insurance policy expired. "I didn't want him to know we didn't have life insurance because of what happened. I didn't want to hear him say 'Grace, it was your fault, because if you hadn't done what you did, I wouldn't have done what I did.'"

They were without insurance for nine months before Grace finally told Harry. In the meantime, she was becoming a media celebrity.

When the domestic violence group near her home found out about what happened with the insurance, they called Congressman Charles Schumer, who decided to make a national issue of it. Melanie Sloan, a lawyer on his staff, conducted her own survey of insurance companies and found that half of the 16 companies she telephoned said they would deny coverage to a woman living in a violent home.

Grace was interviewed by a local TV station, although when the story aired, the station didn't give her real name or show her face: She still didn't want Harry to know.

In March, a month before she had to reapply for insurance, Grace finally told Harry. They were arguing, and at a point during their quarrel, Harry said, "Grace, what else haven't you told me?"

Grace pulled out the tape of the TV story, and after watching it, Harry just sat there shaking his head. It was as if she had dropped a ton of bricks on him.

"Who are you?" Harry asked her, bewildered.

Since then Grace has given lots of interviews and made several public appearances. She has been interviewed on CNN and has been contacted by ABC and NBC. She was invited to Washington, D.C., when President Bill Clinton gave a speech for Mother's Day about health-care reform, and she was there a few weeks ago when Congressman Schumer held a news conference to denounce the insurance companies for discriminating against the victims of domestic violence.

The head lawyer for a leading feminist group threatened to sue the insurance companies if they don't end their discriminatory policies, and Schumer said if they don't stop on their own he would introduce a bill in Congress that would make them stop.

"It's bad enough that women are being battered by their loved ones, but it's even more shocking to discover that they are being battered again by insurance companies," an outraged Schumer said. "Domestic violence is not a pre-existing condition for which coverage may be denied—it's a crime."

Two weeks ago, Grace and Harry got a new insurance policy from State Farm, whose people said since there's been no violence in their home in a year, they are probably a good risk.

And after the public brouhaha, State Farm says it is rethinking its policies on insuring domestic violence victims.

Meanwhile, Grace and Harry still fight, but nobody hits anybody.

"With all these people calling me," Grace said, "it's kept him in shock."

The other night Harry came home and was feeling really mellow. "What's up with you?" Grace said. They sat up until nearly midnight, talking about what had happened to them in the last year.

Harry said: "Why is this happening? Why are all these people calling you? I never thought it would turn into something like this."

"We had a nice conversation," Grace said. "We agreed it was partly my fault because I shoved him first, but we also talked about the man's point of view, that he had a choice to walk away. He said he'll never do it again."

Revolutionary Gesture
JUNE 16, 1993

He was a Supreme Court justice who had come to give a speech. She was a law professor. And I was a lowly law student milling in the crowd that was drawn to his aura.

Professor Ruth Ginsburg walked up to the justice, uttered a greeting that implied familiarity, and straightened his necktie. At the time, the gesture shocked me. The justice's tie didn't even need straightening. Hers was just one of those female gestures that establish intimacy and suggest affection.

Yet this was my law professor, the consummate feminist who didn't equivocate on a single issue concerning the unequal treatment of the sexes. And here she was, fussing with the justice's tie.

That image came back to me when Bill Clinton nominated Ginsburg as the next justice of the Supreme Court. Everybody has described her as shy and quiet, but at the same time as a legal pioneer who is intellectually as tough as nails. It all seems to fit with that vignette of the law professor and the justice.

Professor Ginsburg literally wrote the textbook on sex-discrimination law. The lawbook bore her name, and it was her class on gender-based discrimination that made me stop hating law school and realize I could probably hang in for the full three years.

In class, she was soft-spoken but firm, a feminine woman even with her black hair tied back into a severe bun—and her commitment to the new area of law she was helping to invent was obvious.

I remember one class discussion about whether mothers or fathers had the greater claim to their children in custody disputes. I said I thought an unmarried mother had a superior claim to custody of her child than the child's father, simply by virtue of the fact that she had carried the child and given birth to it. Professor Ginsburg smiled and seemed to find my comment interesting, and while she never said she agreed with me, I sensed that she did. Law professors never answered questions; they asked them.

For credit, I did some research for Professor Ginsburg on a case called *Craig vs. Boren,* which I always referred to as the Oklahoma 3.2 beer case. In that case, which Ginsburg was arguing for the ACLU before the U.S. Supreme Court, two University of Oklahoma fraternity brothers sued that state over a law allowing young women to drink light beer when they were 18, but requiring young men to wait until they were 21. Professor Ginsburg was writing a brief in support of the guys.

My job was to research the question of whether, just because the states traditionally had broad powers to regulate liquor sales, they also had the right to discriminate between males and females in the sale of liquor. I argued that they didn't.

Oklahoma claimed that statistics showed young men were more prone to get drunk, then drive and get into traffic accidents. But in her brief, Ginsburg said the statistics proved no such thing, and that even if they did prove that men and women behaved differently under the influence, you couldn't use those statistics to support a sexually discriminatory law.

She wrote that such laws had no basis in fact, but were based on outdated notions about the way women or men are. Such laws, Ginsburg said, serve only to shore up artificial barriers to full realization by men and women of their human potential, and to retard progress toward equal opportunity free from gender-based discrimination.

Ginsburg told me the *Boren* case was part of a carefully orchestrated legal campaign to get the Supreme Court to treat sexually discriminatory laws the same way it treated racially discriminatory laws. In her *Boren* brief, she argued that the courts would never uphold laws that made distinctions on how different racial groups could drink alcohol, and so shouldn't discriminate between the sexes, either.

Craig vs. Boren was one of five precedent-setting cases Ginsburg won in the Supreme Court during the 1970s—all of which made the courts recognize that sexually discriminatory laws were unconstitutional. The cases were brought when the women's revolution was challenging society's long-held views of what a woman's place was, and they revolutionized the way the courts view gender-based discrimination.

In the cases Ruth Ginsburg argued the Supreme Court struck down state laws that gave men preference over women in administering the estates of their relatives. It held that the families of married women in the military were entitled to the same financial benefits as the families of male military personnel. It struck down Social Security laws that assumed all families were supported by men and then doled out government benefits accordingly. And it ruled that a jury of one's peers meant a jury picked from a pool that included women as well as men.

Ironically, almost all the plaintiffs in the cases were men. It was a clever strategy, arguing that laws which appeared to give special advantages to women in fact hurt women by stereotyping them and confining them to limited roles in society.

Craig vs. Boren was one of the most important cases, since the Supreme Court invented a higher level of scrutiny for state laws that discriminated on the basis of sex.

Before I graduated, Professor Ginsburg gave me a copy of her brief in the *Boren* case—to which I had made a law student's modest contribution of research on a fine point. But in a gracious footnote at the brief's end, she listed the names of the law students who assisted her. The brief is one of my treasured souvenirs.

When President Clinton nominated Professor Ginsburg to the Supreme Court this week, a lot of people talked about her personal reticence and her judicial conservatism. But I think of her as a revolutionary, a woman who could straighten a justice's tie with one hand, and with the other turn the way the law regards women on its head.

Heights' Ugly Secrets
OCTOBER 18, 1993

In the old days, when their love was new, he called her Amira, which to both of them was a term of endearment.

They lived in Colombia and married when she was only 20. In the beginning, their marriage was a beautiful song.

Now he tells the 46-year-old woman who bore his four children that she is no better than a dog. He accuses her of hustling men and calls her the lowest creature on earth. The last time he beat her he bloodied her head and left fist-sized bruises up and down her arm. It is sometimes like this when a marriage goes bad.

A cop gets felled by a flying bucket on the street in Washington Heights or a drug dealer is shot, and the whole world knows about it. But the violence that goes on inside these crowded apartments is the untold story of this neighborhood.

At the beginning of their marriage, they had three good years. Then one day, without telling her, he lent a blanket to a friend. When she realized it was gone, she called the friend and asked for it. This angered her husband, who said, "How dare you call and ask for it when I lent it out?"

He charged at her and she ran with a baby in her arms. Fortunately, when he hit her the grandmother had already grabbed the child. She moved in with her parents, but five days later he apologized, and she came back. There was no more abuse for a while.

Three years later they came to New York and settled in Washington Heights, where arroz con pollo and fried plantains are on the menu of almost every restaurant. Here Amira felt at home among the Dominicans, Mexicans and the other Colombians.

Her husband worked as a porter on the 4 to midnight shift and she had another baby. By now there were four children. One night he came home very late and turned on the stereo. She was in bed with the infant and asked him to lower the music. He lunged for her and chased her around the apartment. He swung at her, but kept missing, until she pushed him and he fell. She fled to a neighbor's apartment and stayed there until he fell asleep. Then she came home.

At a City Council hearing last week for Washington Heights women, the people who run the community agencies said over and over that their clients have more to fear from their husbands' tempers than from anything a drug dealer is likely to do to them on the street.

In Colombia or the Dominican Republic, men have the upper hand and women know their place. When they come to New York, the tables are turned. The men speak no English. They can't find work. Their families live doubled and tripled-up in apartments.

The women generally adjust better, social workers in the neighborhood say. They go to school, learn English, perhaps get a job and become the family breadwinner. They join community associations and attend PTA meetings. Meanwhile, something ugly builds inside the men. They must show the women they are still in charge of the home. So they lunge at the women. It is the volatile mix of machismo and the frustration of the displaced.

At times, Amira's marriage flowed peacefully, and her husband said he was the happiest man on earth. Then he would enter a period of craziness when nothing she did pleased him. Hers was the too-frequent story of the immigrant wife. He didn't want her to work. When she got a job as a seamstress in a factory on 125th Street, he complained that his children were being neglected and that he no longer had a wife. He hounded her until she quit.

She signed up for a class to learn English, but when the young male teacher came to her home to register her, her husband accused her of wanting to have an affair with him. He bought her a set of English-language cassettes instead.

In the 26 years Amira has been married, there were periods of calm, but then her husband would go off again. Usually it happened on his days off, after he'd been drinking. He once beat her with a belt, but most often he used his fists, going for her face. She learned to turn away from him, so that the blows landed on the side of her head. She began to have terrible headaches.

She did not leave him because she is a Spanish-speaking woman in a country where she has no relatives and has only one friend. Because her husband never allowed her to work, she does not know how to earn a living. Most of all she stayed with him because her children loved their father and needed a home. Now they are grown and all but one are gone, and the 25-year-old son who remains tells her she should stop provoking his father.

"What hurts me most," Amira said, "is that I withstood all of this over the years because of my children, and they have turned their backs on me."

The last time her husband beat her, on Sept. 26, he punched her on the head, broke her glasses and threw her across the room. He said he wanted her out of his life and threatened to force her to eat excrement. Since then he has refused to give her money or food. She spends her days in a neighbor's apartment and goes home at night to sleep, maintaining an uneasy truce with her husband.

On the night that Police Officer John Williamson was killed by a blow to his head from a flying bucket of plaster, Amira was nursing a blinding headache from her last beating. When she went home that night she couldn't sleep for the pain. Officer Williamson died at the hospital, his suffering over. Amira tossed on her bed and pondered how she went from being called a beloved one to being called a dog.

United They Stood

JANUARY 8, 1992

They were three little girls in pigtails, sitting on their lunch-boxes during school recess. Their names were Clara, Denise and Andrea. They were 8 years old, in the third grade, and they had decided to form their own club.

They were inspired by their mothers, who belonged to social clubs, with monthly meetings, outings and social activities that were the source of much interest. There on the playground, the Girlies Club was founded.

Their first meeting was at Clara's house. Clara's mother set out a small feast of Moon Pies and milk. The girls ate, elected officers, decided on club dues, took minutes and planned future activities. Clara was elected president, Andrea secretary and Denise treasurer.

Over time, their club grew. At first, all the members lived within two blocks of each other, but soon they began to include girls from other neighborhoods. Club activities were simple. But the meetings—with their business discussions, minutes-taking and refreshments—made them feel grown up.

They planned trips to the movies and the amusement park, threw house parties and organized fund raisers with great seriousness. They once raffled off a cake. Denise and her mother made it from cake mix they bought with club funds, and Denise won the cake.

There was an annual Christmas party, where members wore their best dresses and put on a program. One member would sing, another would play the piano, another would recite a poem. Each gave gifts to the person whose name she had drawn, and they feasted on a Christmas meal bought with club dues and prepared by the mother who was that year's host.

As time went by, clubs became the in thing in their town. Denise and Clara's teenage brothers belonged to the Cavaliers, and wore blue-and-gold sweatshirts and matching hats. They gave dances and were considered very cool. After one Sunday afternoon meeting of the Cavaliers at her house, Clara went into the now-empty living room and smelled the strong, lingering scent of cologne and after-shave. She liked the smell.

When the girls became teenagers, they were embarrassed by the name Girlies Club, so they changed it to the Teenettes. By now, their membership included high school friends from other neighborhoods. The meetings grew more elaborate—they had whole buffets of food. And now they held an annual Christmas dance in a rented hall with a hired band. They wore semi-formals and invited their boyfriends. The parties were lively—and for the most part, they were proper, although a few guests brought liquor and spiked the punch.

In time, Clara, Denise and Andrea went off to college, Clara and Andrea up north and Denise to a small southern school. They kept in touch with the club, though, and at Christmas went to its dances as honored alumnae. But after three or four years, all the members were girls they didn't know, so they finally lost track.

Things began to happen to them. Clara finished college and went to medical school in New York, but she hated what she felt was the sterility of her studies and the ambition of her classmates. To her parents' dismay, she dropped out and went to journalism school instead. She freelanced articles for magazines and got a college job teaching writing. She met a lawyer and married him. Denise was her maid of honor. Andrea had agreed to be a bridesmaid, but she canceled out at the last minute.

Andrea flunked out of college and moved to New York, where she worked as a secretary, took college courses and had an affair with a guy she met on campus. After a while, they broke up. Then Clara and Andrea saw each other often—until Andrea got involved with a religious group that practiced strict dietary laws and preached a philosophy that Clara found bizarre.

One day a couple of years later, Clara saw Andrea approaching her on a Brooklyn street, and she was almost too shocked to speak. Her friend looked as gaunt and wrinkled as a concentration camp survivor. But that was only the beginning of Andrea's downhill slide. She began to call Clara and talk about space creatures who were trying to invade her mind and steal her teeth. She began wandering the streets, talking nonsense. She even set a fire in her apartment. One night when Andrea rang Clara's doorbell, Clara pretended she wasn't in.

After a time, Andrea was admitted to Bellevue, and Clara visited her there, taking her old friend what she'd asked for—some junk food and a few quarters for the pay phone. Andrea's relatives finally took her home to the South, where she spent time in the state mental hospital.

Denise finished graduate school and went to work as a college counselor in Baltimore. She did fine until she was laid off, but then she couldn't find another job. Her parents drove up and took her back down south. For a year or so after that, Denise wrote letters and sent out resumes, but no job materialized. She began to spend her days watching TV. By now, Clara was divorced, but she and Denise kept in touch.

During one holiday, Clara visited Denise, who told her she'd read in the newspaper that the Teenettes had just celebrated their 20th anniversary. They were amazed the club still existed. How did members even know how old the club was? And did they know that Clara and Denise and Andrea were its founders?

During subsequent visits, Clara noticed that Denise was slipping into a world of unreality. She had not held a job in 15 years and when she spoke, she sounded like a child.

During these visits Clara avoided Andrea altogether, unable to deal with her fantasies and occasional outbursts of hostility.

Clara kept working in New York City. Her career prospered, although being on her own in the city sometimes made her lonely. She heard whispers that there were people in her hometown who thought she had squandered her opportunities by not finishing medical school, and that hurt her.

Recently, she visited her parents. She went to see Denise, who seemed to be doing much better. Now, for a change, Denise could hold an intelligent conversation. But Clara felt much closer to Denise's younger sister, a teacher, than she did to her old friend. People told Clara that Andrea was much more lucid these days, especially when she was taking her medication. But Clara didn't bother to visit her.

When she was home, Clara came across a set of photographs of a long-ago Christmas party of the Girlies Club. The three members must have been around 12 at the time, and they were all dressed in their best clothes. Clara was wearing a pretty red and white dress, and white bows dangled from her two pigtails. In spite of the fond memories, the pictures made Clara feel a little sad.

Denise's sister told Clara she'd heard that the Teenettes gave a Christmas dance this year. After all these years the club is still going strong.

Making Women Single-Minded

JULY 14, 1993

When Desiree Lopez of the Bronx had a baby at age 16, marrying the father wasn't even a question in her mind.

"My mother told him I was pregnant, and he said he couldn't take care of our baby because he already had one. I didn't even know about the other baby."

She dumped the boyfriend fast, and in spite of premature motherhood, went on with her life. She's trying to finish high school and dreams of going to college and becoming a doctor some day.

She might even like to have another child, when she's older and better prepared. But she doesn't dream of marriage.

"No," Desiree says. "Because men are dogs. They go out with you and you find out they're going out with somebody else. They're not dependable."

According to the U.S. Census Bureau, girls like Desiree are the wave of the future. The census study found that the number of never-married mothers is increasing across the board— among all economic groups, all races, all educational levels, and in every part of the country.

We already knew that the unwed motherhood rate was highest among females who hadn't finished high school. What's news is that the percentage of never-married mothers with high school diplomas has almost doubled in the last decade, while it has more than doubled among women with one year or more of college.

Black women still have the highest percentage of out-of-wedlock birth (two-thirds of all black births), but the numbers are up for Hispanic and white women as well. For black women, we already knew the reason was that there are no men to marry—not enough black men with jobs and too many who are in jail or on drugs. We knew there was a problem with black men. Now we're learning that there's a problem with all men.

One reason there are so many more unmarried mothers is that single motherhood is tolerated more than it used to be. At one time, a woman who got pregnant before marriage was either locked away or shamed in public. Now families and society in general are more tolerant, and schools encourage pregnant girls to stay in school. Another reason is the economic climate—increasing job insecurity has led men to shun the economic responsibilities of marriage.

Some say it's because more women postponed motherhood in order to advance their careers—so they're now having children on their own because at their age there are no more eligible males. I know the first part of this proposition is untrue, since every career woman I've ever known was looking for a husband all along, and just couldn't find anyone decent who wanted to marry her. "It may be it's becoming harder and harder for people to connect in a very profound, intimate way," says Ruth Sidel, a sociologist who's made a study of young women and their expectations.

"I'm concerned about what's happening in the New York City swimming pools—the baiting and harassing of women as the way men bond with women . . . If a lot of the interaction between the sexes is just power trips or sex, then you're not likely to end up married."

For her book, *On Her Own: Growing Up in the Shadow of the American Dream,* Sidel interviewed young women between 14 and 24 and was surprised to discover they had a John Wayne, horse-on-a-frontier, doing-battle-alone mentality.

It's about young women feeling they have to make it on their own, that there are no men out there, that they can't count on their families. They feel they have to make their own careers and they don't believe they'll be able to connect with people.

Many are hoping to marry and make the storybook kind of marriage, but aren't at all sure it's going to work. They felt they were individuals alone in this huge sea, having to make their own way in life.

A lot of men have the attitude that it's fine to sire a child, but they aren't much interested in the responsibilities of raising and supporting one. The family-values people can say what they will, but in real life, even married women complain about having to function as if they were single parents.

So more and more women are like Cheryle Ludlum, who had a child at 16, was married briefly and divorced in her 20s, and in her 40s decided to adopt another child.

"It would be nice to be able to have a husband," says Cheryle, (who didn't remarry because there wasn't anyone out there to be married to), "but if you can't, why should you waste that emotion . . . when you have other options. We would all like everything to be fairy-tale perfect—but let's face it: There are simply not enough men to go around."

The Census Bureau figures are alarming, not because there are so many never-married mothers (many of them get along just fine), but because of the underlying reasons for it:

- The epidemic of teenage pregnancy, its explanation still a mystery in this era of available birth control.
- The joblessness of black men and the racism that underlies it.
- The inability of men and women to make connections.
- The storybook vision girls once had of their lives hasn't just been tarnished. It's been blasted to shreds.

Pieces of Memories

FEBRUARY 14, 1994

They were together in the hospital, the old lovers, united in their recognition of an old melody.

She was the sick one. She lay crumpled in a permanent fetal position; no more than 90 pounds, if that. Her body was wasted by a stroke and her mind by the Alzheimer's disease that had come before.

Yet it was obvious that she had once been lovely. There was the delicate face, the huge, oval eyes, the white hair twisted into a long braid on the side. He sat at her bedside, a slight, gray-haired man of 75, sweet-looking in his tweed jacket. They looked like figures out of a miniature oil painting.

He told my friend, who was in the bed next to his wife's, that this was his second marriage, and the happy one. His mother had loved his wife. She thought she would make him save money. In his youth he had been frivolous. He used to dance a lot, especially the rumba.

Now he was confused about everything that was happening in his life. Three or four times a day he would telephone the hospital room.

"I'm looking for my wife," he told my friend.

"She can't talk right now because she's sleeping."

"Where is she?" he would ask, and my friend told him his wife was in the hospital. They would go over the address of the hospital and the room number several times.

"I'll come over tomorrow, he said, because it's too late now." It was only 7 o'clock in the morning.

He had been a professor, he said, and she was a teacher. One could see a gentleness in her demeanor that would have been appropriate with children. They had no kids of their own, so she became his child, and he hers.

When they got married they lived in lower Manhattan. They belonged to the crowd that frequented places such as Town Hall and City Center and lived lives of quiet gentility. They made a lot of money and, as his mother had hoped, the wife made him save it. Twenty-five years ago they bought a house near the seashore.

"You must come and visit," he told my friend.

He came to see his wife, who's in her late 60s, three times a week. He would stay for an hour, holding her hand, cooing to her. He would look at her and call her endearing names. "You're my baby," he'd say. "You're my life."

She communicated with him through looks. She would open her eyes or close them. She would look at him and make faces. Her recognition of him was not as strong as it was with the nurses and doctors who tended her every day, but perhaps she had an inkling that he was someone she had once known.

Both of them were lost. "Where am I?" he would ask whenever he came. "What's this building?"

They were like many couples their age, men and women who were once each other's lover, husband, wife, boyfriend, girlfriend, antagonist, business partner; couples who had shared a rich history, but now could summon up only bits and pieces of it.

Still, they were more fortunate than some couples, who had already been separated in different nursing homes, and who were no longer aware of the whereabouts or even the existence of the other. Still other couples had been parceled out among their various children, never to see each other again.

For now, at least, these old lovers were still together, although the threads that bound them were growing thinner by the day.

"That's the sad thing about Alzheimer's," my friend said. "With other diseases you can at least remember the nice things that happened to you. You can still feel rage that you've been cheated. You can cry over your losses. But this disease robs you of your history."

Soon she would be going into a nursing home, and he would be left to fend for himself. When they were last seen, he was sitting by her bedside, still trying to make a connection, smiling at his baby, his life.

Chapter 3

Lawyers, rubbers and football heroes: A reasonable expectation of justice

Confessions of a *"Court TV"* Addict

JUNE 22, 1994

Mickey Sherman is spinning out of control.

This became clear to him two years ago when he was dining out with his wife and a couple of friends. One of the friends was Michael Bolton, he of the leonine hair and faux-soul recordings, and the other was Bolton's pal, Nicolette Sheridan.

They were sitting in a restaurant eating when all of a sudden three couples came in, and one of the guys looked at Mickey and said: "My God, that's Mickey Sherman of 'Court TV'!"

They were gaping and pointing at Mickey and the guy came over and introduced him to his party, while Bolton and Sheridan looked on in amazement.

"What am I, chopped liver?" Bolton later asked.

It is sometimes like this when you become a "Court TV" lawyer. People start staring and pointing and you can no longer give the finger to someone who cuts you off in your convertible, because you have ceased to be just some guy, and have become that guy on "Court TV."

It is my opinion that almost everyone in the world wants to be on television. The idea of having 15 million people listen to your fleeting thoughts is thrilling enough to make a surgeon abandon his operating theater. You can spend 20 years repairing tendons and muscles in obscurity, but a 15-second sound bite will turn you into a household word.

Watching lawyers get the TV bug is not a pretty sight. Catherine Crier deserted her Texas judicial bench for CNN and then network stardom. Star Jones left the Brooklyn DA's office for a hot minute as a "Court TV" reporter before going to the network, and she now has her own syndicated show. And with all his television projects, they can't keep law professor Arthur Miller at Harvard anymore.

Much of lawyering is tedious, while television is just fun.

"What could be easier than sitting there pontificating about other lawyers' performances?" says Sherman, a former prosecutor and public defender turned criminal defense lawyer.

"I feel I'm on the fringe of journalism, and it's doing something other than helping people who are accused of horrendous crimes remain at liberty."

Mickey Sherman receives resumes from lawyers, police officers and others who want to know how they can get on TV. Melvin Belli has tried repeatedly to get on "Court TV" as a guest commentator, but he is not considered up to snuff. The network's producers say they prefer Myrna Felder, a divorce attorney, to her husband, Raoul.

Sherman has been on "Court TV" maybe 200 times, including last week, when he was invited to do live commentary on O.J. Simpson's flight from the LAPD and his arraignment on Monday.

It was like virtual news, he said, very exciting.

Nobody thought much about "Court TV" when it got started in 1991, and even trial lawyers thought televised court cases would send viewers into a coma. But soap operas like the William Kennedy Smith rape trial sucked viewers in, and "Court TV" trials are grittier and less predictable than the daily talk shows and soap operas.

Yes, my name is Sheryl McCarthy, and I am a "Court TV" addict.

I have lain awake in an insomniac haze, stunned as I watched a parade of adults tell the former Rev. James Porter, a Catholic priest who molested them as children, that he had earned a place in hell. I have rooted for Claire Maglica to win her palimony battle against millionaire flashlight tycoon Tony Maglica, with whom she lived for 23 years.

I was delighted to see Weldon Wayne Carr, who set his house on fire with his wife inside it, found guilty of murder. And I was pleased when a lone juror held out against convicting a young man accused of shooting some young thugs who tried to run him down in a truck.

Watching a trial day by day gives you a different understanding of it than you could ever get from reading about it in the newspaper. Victims and alleged perps become people, not symbols. It is real life—and there is justice, but there is also stupidity and confusion.

You learn that the court system works much better than you thought it did, and that the verdicts are more carefully considered than you expected from hearing about them in a vacuum.

"Court TV" commentators have told me that having cameras in courtrooms makes the trial system work better. Judges start trials on time. The lawyers arguing the trials do their homework, are more courteous, and try to do the best possible job, because they don't want to look like jerks in front of 15 million people.

Of course, if you're a trial lawyer, being a commentator on "Court TV" can also be great for business. "People seem to place greater value on my services simply because I'm on television," Sherman says.

"I don't think being glib in front of a camera has anything to do with legal ability. I don't know that the public appreciates that, but I'm certainly not complaining."

It also helps one get reservations at restaurants.

Sherman would even consider doing TV full time, if given the right opportunity. He's done other TV shows as a result of his appearances on "Court TV." He is fascinated by TV production, has earned some script credits, and has had a trial he argued on "Court TV" nominated for an award for documentaries.

"It's absurd that I'm not talking about Supreme Court cases or search-and-seizure issues," Sherman says, "but about categories for TV awards. It's obvious that I'm out of control."

Blinded by Brilliance
JUNE 20, 1994

In his glory days O.J. Simpson would run to daylight, breaking past dangerous men with his blood in their eyes, to set new records.

Later he dashed through airports, in fantastical recreations of his football exploits that made us laugh.

Last week on a California freeway he was running again; only this time he was running towards the abyss.

It had taken courage to run against men who were twice his

size. It took no courage at all to murder the mother of two children and her companion, if in fact he was the one who did it. And it took no courage to repeatedly beat and terrorize the same woman, which we know for a certainty that he did.

Despite records and trophies and certification as a hero in the Football Hall of Fame, O.J. Simpson's last run was the running of a coward. Rumors of bloody gloves and ski masks notwithstanding, these reports could have been bogus. Not even the announcement that he had been formally charged with murder (which could have been a mistake) indicted him in my mind so much as the sight of O.J. Simpson in flight.

A man who is certain of his innocence has no need to flee, especially when the whole world, including the police who are investigating you, want to be believe you are blameless.

We loved Simpson's smooth facade, his handsomeness, his incredible prowess in sports, his pleasantness. We also compensate for the bad things athletes do because they are so awesome on the field. We look at their athletic deeds, not at their lives.

A man I know tells me that men see the playing field as a metaphor for life. Men put a lot of their understanding of the world in how you play the game, he says. When O.J. broke away into an 80-yard run, or caught a touchdown, it was as if you were doing it. You were winning. If he's screwed up monumentally now, it means all the things that accrued to you from him all those years were bogus.

Women also can be crazed over star athletes, but also size them up in terms of their family and interpersonal relationships. One woman I know, who was once married to a member of the New York Jets, talked about the thrill of going with the team to the Super Bowl. She also described the terror of having her husband hold a gun to her head for hours, and of being chased naked into the street.

The weakness in O.J. Simpson's character that is coming to light now was surely there all along, and certainly flared up long before we ever heard about it. Marguerite Simpson, the first wife whom he left for Nicole, and who has been tastefully silent through this recent trouble, could have stories to tell.

After Simpson pleaded no contest to charges of beating up

Nicole Simpson in 1989, he didn't miss a beat in his contracts with NBC or with Hertz. Had he still been playing football, he could have been suspended. In the corporate world's view, he was still running touchdowns.

But a couple of dead bodies will trip up the most skillful of running backs. Now, as more dirt dribbles out on O.J., his accomplishments are becoming smaller and his life is becoming larger.

The thousands who cheered him on the Los Angeles overpasses didn't seem to realize it, though. They acted like he was still running to daylight.

More attention should have been paid to Simpson's life. If he'd done the 30 days in jail the district attorney asked for in 1989 after he beat up Nicole, if his contracts had been canceled, maybe he wouldn't be sitting in a jail cell right now.

The Press Should Arrest Itself

JUNE 29, 1994

The Los Angeles Police Department's decision to release the tapes of Nicole Simpson's 1993 police calls is one of the most outrageous acts it has committed in handling the O.J. Simpson murder case.

People can expound all they want about the First Amendment and the public's right to know, but nothing rationalizes away the injustice done to Simpson by releasing these tapes.

If you put these principles on a scale against Simpson's right to a fair trial, the public's right to hear the tapes winds up having the heft of feather.

On one hand is satisfying the public's curiosity. On the other hand is a man's life.

I was riveted to my TV set when I first heard the 911 tapes, and I have heard them a half-dozen times since. They are dramatic truth-telling, and they have the added benefit of being real.

The tapes made great TV more compelling because they came in the midst of a dry broadcast season. But I should never have been given a chance to hear them, certainly not before the murder case came to trial.

If the nation could not fathom the idea of O.J. Simpson's slashing two people to death because he wasn't the type, the tapes told us in his own blood-chilling words that he may very well have been the type. What could be more prejudicial to his case than hearing him threaten to harm the woman he is now accused of murdering?

Releasing these tapes was the tail-end of a procession of half-truths, rumors and innuendoes that were tossed to the press and gobbled up pretty much the way dogs gobble scraps from the dinner table.

It is a well-known habit of police to lie and manufacture evidence, yet the press has passed along whatever was tossed our way. Bloody gloves and bloody footprints have been offered as proof that Simpson did it, along with a ski mask and a army-style shovel tool no one has actually seen. The tapes were the latest, choicest morsel, and the press pounced on them like red meat.

The police leaked rumors and the press reported them. And the district attorney, who is running for re-election, became a talk-show regular and allowed the police to release the tapes. Then he held a news conference to say that releasing the tapes was prejudicial to his case. The man should be in jail.

You know things are bad when the most avid defenders of press freedom start to gag. "I was appalled when the tapes were released," says Vivian Berger, chief counsel for the American Civil Liberties Union, which is always staring down some other group in defense of the First Amendment. "My instinct is for the public to know and for nothing to be suppressed . . . But here there's a very strong competing right."

"The sleazification of the media is almost total at this point," says Stephen Isaacs, acting dean of the Columbia University Graduate School of Journalism. "All people know is what they've learned from the media, which means they don't know a thing. The media has thrown away all the precepts of journalism."

There was a time when newspapers and broadcast networks promised not to behave this way. In 1954, an osteopath named Sam Sheppard was convicted of murdering his wife.

This happened at the end of a trial in which reporters eaves-dropped on conversations between Sheppard and his attorney, witnesses gave interviews to the press, and a TV helicopter circled overhead when the jury went to visit the scene of the murder.

When the U.S. Supreme Court overturned Sheppard's conviction, citing the press' behavior, the media experienced once of their rare moments of shame. Editors and broadcasters drew up guidelines on how they would cover trials in the future.

They would report the basic facts of a case before a trial, they said, but they would not report such things as whether the defendant had confessed or given a statement, or whether the defendant had a criminal record.

The news media pretty much abided by these rules until 1981, when a judge in a Washington state murder trial threatened to bar reporters from pre-trial hearings unless they promised to abide by their own rules.

The journalists balked. Then another judge said the rules were merely voluntary, and that the previous judge had no right to hold them to their own policies. Since then, we of the press have regressed almost to where we were during the Sheppard trial.

We are so worried that someone else will break a story we don't have that we write about nonexistent ski masks and run transcriptions of broadcast tapes that could damn a man before he even gets to trial. The press put on its brakes once before. It's time we experienced a new attack of shame.

Tyson Was KO'd
FEBRUARY 17, 1993

Her lips said no, no, but her eyes said yes, yes.

So goes the latest argument by attorney Alan Dershowitz, as he explained to an appeals court this week why Mike Tyson deserves a new trial in the rape case of Desiree Washington.

According to Dershowitz, trial judge Patricia Gifford erred

by not telling the jury it shouldn't find Tyson guilty if he misconstrued Washington's cries of No to mean Yes. Anybody can make a mistake.

Dershowitz is hard to take even on a good day. When he's being flagrantly sexist and smug, he's impossible. But what can you expect from a man who has taken to prostituting his legal brilliance in the service of the amoral wealthy? In recent history, he has defended the likes of Claus von Bulow, Leona Helmsley, Michael Milken, and now Mike Tyson.

Dershowitz says he takes on unpopular clients to protect them from abuses of the law and the Constitution. He really takes them on for the notoriety and the cash. Clearly he fancies himself a modern-day Clarence Darrow, and it boosts his ego to prove that he can get off the un-get-offable.

I remember waiting in line outside a Manhattan theater to see a movie about the von Bulow case. Dershowitz was in line too, and appeared to be absolutely hyperactive at the prospect of seeing himself on the screen. The von Bulow reversal was one of his better-justified victories. As he himself said, "Just because you wished your wife dead doesn't mean you killed her."

At a gathering over the weekend, I heard a man say of the Tyson conviction. "I still think there was something funny about that case. Whenever it's one person's word against another's, you can never know."

Here we go again, I thought, knowing that Tyson's appeal and the new TV documentary about his life will start people picking over the bones of Tyson versus Washington. The man was right. You can rarely know anything with absolute certainty. Even when you do—as in the beating of Rodney King by four L.A. police officers—the jury's verdict may astonish you. But the fact that you don't know with scientific certainty doesn't mean you can't make a sound and reasoned judgment. Otherwise not even the most heinous criminals would ever get put away.

Mike Tyson practically admitted he forced himself on Desiree Washington. At trial, it was: "She knew I was a sex maniac, but she came to my room anyway." Now it's: "She said no, but I figured she really meant yes."

Dredging up the Mike Tyson case is a mistake. But I guess it's just too painful for some people to let Mike Tyson stay in jail. It's painful for people like the Rev. T.J. Jemison and a group of black Baptist ministers who, promised a large sum of money by Tyson, could utter a communal prayer for him but not for Desiree Washington.

It's painful for those in the fight business who are losing money as long as Tyson stays behind bars. This includes people like Tyson's manager Don King and Donald Trump, who tried to buy off a jail term by proposing to the judge that Tyson start a fund to help rape victims.

In the new Tyson documentary, there are videos of a different Tyson from the one we know. He is a cute and charming adolescent—sympathetic, childlike and vulnerable. The movie dispels what has become legend, that Tyson was doing fine as long as Cus D'Amato was alive and kept him in check, but that after D'Amato died, Tyson went out of control. According to the film, D'Amato didn't set boundaries for Tyson either. When one of D'Amato's trainers suspended Tyson from the gym for lewdly propositioning a young girl, D'Amato fired the guy and overruled the suspension. When you've got a potential heavyweight champion on your hands, rules fly out the window.

There shouldn't be a new trial because, as the prosecutor says, he did it. It would also dredge up a panoply of fears and suspicions—about women who falsely accuse men of rape, about whites who want to ruin powerful black men, about grudge matches between black men and black women. This is one case where such suspicions were simply overridden by the facts.

Watching the old movie clips, I was charmed by Mike Tyson. He was talented and physically beautiful. I could feel for him. But the new Mike Tyson is cool and cocky. Too cocky to apologize for what happened with Desiree Washington. Too cool to entertain the idea that he did anything wrong. His excuse is: She said no, but he heard yes.

Mike Tyson doesn't need a new trial. He needs to stay in jail a while longer, until he learns a few things.

William Kuntsler and the "Black Rage" Defense

MARCH 28, 1994

When Colin Ferguson got beat up by a bunch of inmates in jail last week, aside from his lawyers, nobody much cared.

Never mind that the beating was almost certainly a set-up that required the cooperation of a prison guard or two. A broken nose and a black eye on a guy who shot up a trainload of people seemed like a minor example of jailhouse justice.

What was remarkable was the sudden change the attack seemed to bring about in Ferguson's attitude. "I have no hostility toward anyone," he told reporters. "There's always room for disagreement. We can always absorb conflict without inflicting wounds and injury to anyone."

The discovery of this schizophrenic Colin Ferguson, who rages at whites, Asians and Uncle Tom blacks in one breath, and in the next breath calls for racial harmony, is our latest proof that Ferguson represents absolutely no one but himself.

Recently his lawyers, William Kunstler and Ron Kuby, announced their plan to argue a black rage defense at Ferguson's murder trial. This defense says that Ferguson was so tormented by racism that it made him crazy and drove him to shoot those people on the Long Island Rail Road.

The reaction to this was not good. "Black rage?" one guard later told Ferguson. "I'll show you some white rage!"

The guard is not alone in mocking Kunstler and Kuby's legal strategy.

"It's a specious argument," said a friend of mine, who is black. "It's a liberal thing from the '60s that says we are not responsible for our actions because the state has beat us down. So we, the lawyers, have to protect you. It's a kind of condescension that I cannot stomach."

Kunstler says he got the black rage idea from reading an advertisement for a book by Ellis Cose, a black journalist. *The Rage of a Privileged Class* is about the anger experienced by middle-class blacks, who play by society's rules but still find themselves shut out of jobs and promotions, denied loans and passed up by cab drivers.

"I have my doubts as to whether he [Kunstler] has read my book," Cose told me.

There's certainly a lot of anger among blacks, and that includes blacks who are middle class, as Colin Ferguson was. But there's also a lot of mental illness. . . . I certainly haven't written a book about black sociopaths.

Here are some problems with the black rage defense:

- It equates the behavior of a sociopath, Colin Ferguson, to the behavior of all blacks, most of whom live productive and law-abiding lives despite whatever anger they may feel at society's injustice. It reduces their justified rage and frustration to the level of the Twinkie Defense.

- It sounds shamelessly liberal and condescending, by trying to absolve a villain/mental case of responsibility for his grossly antisocial behavior.

- Kunstler and Kuby, who have done a lot of good in their legal careers, have also gotten some really bad guys off the hook by using the victim-of-society theory.

- It sounds too much like the child-abuse defense in the Menendez brothers trial. It tries to excuse a heinous crime by blaming a social ill. While we recognize that child abuse and racism are terrible things, we suspect they weren't the real reason Ferguson or the Menendez brothers did what they did.

Yet, depending on who's on the jury, the black rage defense might prove to be effective for Colin Ferguson.

"I think it's brilliant defense," says Michael Gross, a criminal lawyer who thinks racism is a disease that can make its victims engage in aberrant conduct.

Kunstler has taught us a lot of things. In his hands or Ron Kuby's hands, this theory has a real opportunity to be developed.

Writer Cose doesn't agree: "I can't understand how it makes sense as a legal strategy. If he's trying to make an insanity defense, he should make it as specific to Ferguson and his situation as possible, and not generalize to a rage that's felt by millions of people."

Cose learned from researching his book that while most blacks recognize there's a lot of anger among blacks and understand why that is, it's not something most whites want to deal with.

It would be a shame if Colin Ferguson's irrational anger and tragic behavior became confused with the kind of anger most blacks feel every day, without ever taking a gun to anybody.

A Silence in L.A.

APRIL 19, 1993

After the verdicts were read, after the courtroom was cleared and the lawyers interviewed, after cheers had been heard in some quarters and slow shakes of the head were seen in others, there was nothing but silence.

For weeks, there had been speculation about how high things were going to blow if the four cops were let off again this time. But the jury came back and announced that two of the cops were convicted and two were acquitted, and yet all you heard in Los Angeles was quiet.

There are those who say there were no riots this time because the blacks of L.A. got what they wanted: two cops convicted and vengeance for the beating of Rodney King. They say the threat of more riots was like a gun held to the head of the criminal justice system, and that Laurence Powell and Stacey Koon were sacrificial offerings to an angry community.

But last spring's riots didn't occur just because the verdict didn't go the way blacks wanted. And the calm after Saturday's verdict wasn't just because they got their way this time. You saw the interviews. Plenty of people felt that all four cops should have been convicted, but said they could live with the verdict nonetheless. If the verdict still left the black community's glass half-empty, why didn't L.A. explode again?

We know from experience that juries can come up with some surprising verdicts. The criminal justice system is infected with biases of all kinds—economic, sexual, racial, religious. We know we won't always get justice from the system, but we accept it because we feel we have a reasonable expectation of justice.

An Indiana jury convicts Mike Tyson of rape, which is taken by some as a racist verdict, yet a series of New York juries acquit Larry Davis, a drug dealer, a likely murder and a truly bad man, of murder and attempted murder. The system is racist, some complain, but if so then why does Davis, a black man, get off? A jury in New York City acquits a bunch of St. John's University athletes of raping a young woman, but a jury in Glen Ridge, N.J., convicts a bunch of former high school athletes of raping a mentally retarded girl. The system is sexist, we say, but then why do the Glen Ridge boys get the boot? A jury acquits Lemrick Nelson of murdering Yankel Rosenbaum during the Crown Heights riot in Brooklyn, while a prosecutor decides not to press charges against Yosef Lifsh, the driver of the car that killed Gavin Cato, which touched off the riot in Crown Heights in the first place. Does this mean the system is anti-black or anti-Jewish?

With every verdict someone is aggrieved because they feel the decision should have gone their way. Some jury verdicts are just plain wrong, but we can accept them as long as they are not outrageously wrong, and as long as they don't insult our reasonable expectation of getting justice from the court system.

The riots in L.A. didn't occur simply because blacks in the first trial of the cops who beat Rodney King didn't get the verdict they thought they should have gotten. The riots occurred because that verdict was an affront to their expectation of justice. The silence in Los Angeles over the last weekend was not the result of black residents' feeling they'd been vindicated because the policemen were finally convicted of something. It was because the jury's verdict was a reasonable one, and assured them that while they might not like every jury's verdict, they can at least have a reasonable expectation of getting justice from the system.

The beauty of this jury's verdict is in its imperfection—two convicted, two acquitted. Justice is not always a matter of all or nothing. Sometimes it is complex. If the jury could convict Laurence Powell, who landed most of the 56 blows on Rodney

King, and Stacey Koon, the commanding officer who let him do it, then L.A. residents could accept the jury's decision that Theodore Briseno may have tried to stop the beating and that Timothy Wind may have been a scared rookie.

The verdict may not have totally pleased them, but at least it struck them as reasonable. It made them feel they have a reasonable shot at justice from this system, and not just an expectation of insult.

This explains the silence of Los Angeles.

Cop Thugs Had it Easier
SEPTEMBER 29, 1993

"People are sick of this riot stuff," one disgusted reporter said in the courtroom where they are wrapping up the trial of Damian Williams and Henry Keith Watson.

"Over at my office they're not interested in it," a magazine writer added.

The trial of these two young men has been a quiet trial. The reporters and the cameras are here, and even a few civilians come by the courthouse trying to get in. But if you compare the decibel level of this trial to that of the cops who were tried for beating Rodney King, this trial sounds like a whisper.

"It's just a trial of some people who did something wrong," said Michael Boyd, 46, who was waiting at the courthouse to see if he'd be called to serve on a jury in another case.

"It has no social significance whatsoever."

After the Los Angeles riots, the beating of Reginald Denny became, in the public eye, the counterpoint to the beating of Rodney King. If the world was outraged by the injustice of the cops' first acquittal, it was also appalled at the beating of Reginald Denny as a form of revenge.

But now the trial of Damian Williams and Henry Keith Watson seems to have lost its cachet. Now it's just a trial of two thugs who used a riot as an excuse to be themselves.

Williams and Watson are a pair of punks. The array of evidence and witnesses presented by the prosecutors leave little doubt about the viciousness with which they behaved on that April day in 1992 at the corner of Florence and Normandie Avenues in South Central Los Angeles.

But this trial is about more than the actions of two punks. It's about a justice system that has once again tumbled over the edge.

This began when Williams and Watson were overcharged for their crimes. The attacks on Denny and seven others at that intersection that day were vicious and inexcusable. But the young men caught up in a riot that was sparked by another injustice might more reasonably have been charged with assault with a deadly weapon, instead of attempted murder.

To set their bail at more than a half million dollars, forcing them to remain in jail for 16 months prior to the trial, was unnecessary. These were neighborhood guys, after all. Where were they going to flee to?

Compare this with Federal Judge John Davies' decision to undersentence the cops, Stacey Koon and Laurence Powell, and to allow them to stay out of jail pending appeals. This increased the sense of bias in the way the two cases were handled.

This week Judge Davies struck again, giving Koon and Powell, who had already shown up to begin serving their prison time, two more weeks of freedom, while they file another appeal.

The problem with this case is that two opposing forces are at work. The first is that Williams and Watson are criminals who ought to do some time. The second is that they also were discriminated against in the filing of the charges.

By being overzealous in trying to get them, the prosecutors and former L.A. police chief Daryl Gates muddied the waters of the case.

Now many of the blacks in Los Angeles can see only bias, and not justice, at work in this courtroom, as in the first trial when Koon and Powell were acquitted.

It would have been so easy to treat this case with common sense and moderation. Instead we may have two young men who are rightfully sent to jail, but a large part of a community will still feel that it has been mugged.

The Jury from Hell

OCTOBER 19, 1993

Early on, it looked like the jury from hell.

One juror, light-headed with drink, regaled his neighbors nightly with tales from the courtroom. The trial gave him his 15 minutes of fame, and he used them. He passed around news clippings about the case, and he announced the verdict weeks before the attorneys rested their case.

The judge deep-sixed him before the deliberations began.

Then there was Juror 104. The stress of deliberating sent her running down a hallway screaming and cursing. She wanted to see her boyfriend, and being sequestered was a drag. A day off with her paramour calmed her down. A little sex can have beneficial effects on a jury, too.

Two more jurors were excused for health reasons, and another, a fundamentalist Christian, was let go for personal reasons. There was also the sad spectacle of Juror 373, the Twilight Zone juror. She existed on a mental plane of her own, her colleagues said.

Jurors were dropping so fast one wondered if they were making up ailments and feigning nervous breakdowns to get out of deciding this case. But then, being in a jury room can turn you around 180 degrees and make you a different person from the one you were when you went in.

I was on a jury once, deciding a case involving two young men from Harlem. One shot the other over a bit of trivia and faced a murder rap. On the first vote, I was ready to convict him of second-degree murder. "Haul him away and lock him up for a long time," I said.

Then came nudgings from the other jurors. There was the elderly woman, cautious and kindly, who didn't want to see two men's lives wasted. There was the guy who was sick of the trial and wanted to go home; he was ready to strike any compromise to get out of the jury room. There was the young woman who believed we should convict the young man of murder—and was tortured by the idea of showing any leniency. The other jurors reasoned with her, and she slowly changed, but reluctantly and tearfully. In the end, I voted with the others for second-degree manslaughter and felt just fine about it.

Most juries work hard, and most jurors are fired by a sense of responsibility to the public and the defendant. In a system filled with opposing attorneys and judges, expert witnesses and jurors all trying to do the right thing, it is hard to convict anyone of a crime. That is the flawed beauty of the jury system.

By yesterday, the crazed jury from hell in Los Angeles had returned a piecemeal verdict that was wiser than anything the calm and smug jurors of Simi Valley were able to produce. They convicted Damian Williams and Henry Watson of being rioters, assaulters and punks—but they also seem poised to say that they were not the aspiring murderers that prosecutors claimed they were.

It was mayhem and it was a riot and the two men acted abominably, but the jury rejected the prosecution's overcharging of them. "They came back with a verdict that says these men intended to assault and riot, but that's all," said Michael Ross, a former New York City prosecutor who is now a defense lawyer.

The jurors lived under a lot of pressure and it showed. The woman who ran through the hallway ran because she felt the pressure, and the judge properly concluded that you don't have to be crazy to run through the hallway. Sometimes when you're a juror, you just feel like running through the hallway.

Sometimes juries screw up, but the genius of the system was played out in this case. With all the political pressures on them, the thousands of pages of testimony, the conflicting experts, the burden of another potential riot and the hot breath of the press on their necks, these jurors came as close to justice as we could have hoped.

Chapter 4

No books,
no brains,
no chance

The Other School Violence

JANUARY 12, 1994

This is the story of LaQuinn Evans, 15, a Harlem youngster, and the violence that was inflicted on him in a New York City public school over some textbooks.

In the fall of 1991, LaQuinn was a seventh-grader at the A. Phillip Randolph School for Science and Technology on West 120th Street. The school was really part of the old Wadleigh Junior High, but the students and their parents had been promised an exciting, new and stimulating curriculum. Along with those promises the school got a fancy new name. It became the rather lofty sounding School for Science and Technology.

LaQuinn was an average student who had suffered from a speech impediment since he was in the third grade. But his real problems didn't start, his mother says, until he was a seventh grader.

"He started coming home with a lot of papers, xerox copies of the homework he was supposed to do," Stephanie Evans said.

"I asked where were his textbooks. He said he didn't have any. The xeroxed papers were incomplete. We could hardly read them. It was awful and when I went to the school to complain, they said they xeroxed so much stuff that the copier was constantly breaking down."

The school's director—all the fancy new schools have directors instead of principals—told Mrs. Evans that while the school had textbooks, it didn't have enough for all the students. So for the time being they were photocopying lessons and passing them out to everyone. He promised her he was doing everything he could to get some textbooks soon.

By March, 1992, LaQuinn still had no books. By now he was barely passing his courses and had begun to speak of his school with derision.

"He said it wasn't even a school, that it was a joke," Mrs. Evans said. "I told him even though the situation was like that, he should try to make the best of it."

Evans found a tutor for LaQuinn, Dr. E. Babette Edwards,

who runs the Harlem Tutorial and Referral Project on West 125th Street. Edwards was appalled to learn that LaQuinn didn't have a single textbook on any subject. So she wrote to Board of Ed President Carl McCall to complain.

McCall called for an investigation into the matter by officials at the Board of Education. At first, the district superintendent, Anton Klein, told the investigator that LaQuinn had all the necessary textbooks. But Klein lied.

Later his deputy admitted to board officials that, indeed, the boy had no books. In April, seven months into the school year, Klein told the investigator that the reason the school had no textbooks was that the school's director hadn't submitted the purchase orders required to get them. Klein promised he would make sure this was done right away.

Mrs. Evans said LaQuinn finally brought some textbooks home in June. School let out for the summer near the end of that month.

According to Dr. Edwards, LaQuinn's story is not uncommon, especially in poor and minority neighborhoods around the city. Every week, she says, she hears complaints from parents of students who have no textbooks to bring home.

"A teacher at another school in Harlem told me books are too valuable for children to take home. I reminded her that the children are also valuable."

"It's an intolerable situation we have in these schools," Dr. Edwards said. "It can't go on. These communities are disintegrating around us, and one reason is grossly inadequate schools."

The recent trend in New York City has been to create lots of minischools with exciting names and promises of creative new curricula that give parents hopes—often false ones—that their children's education is going to improve. How much science or technology or reading can be taught without books?

Yesterday, prominent men in our government testified at a hearing downtown, where they decried the fact that far too many kids are being sucked into lives of crime and despair that short-circuit their futures and plague the lives of others. They resolved to do whatever is possible to end this cycle of violence.

But what of the violence that was done to LaQuinn Evans, who slowly came to believe that school was a joke because what was a school without books?

He totally lost interest in school during the seventh grade, his mother said. "Sometimes when I get angry with him and try to get him focused, he tells me, 'This is no school. The teachers are not teaching us,' and things like that.'"

Last fall LaQuinn entered the ninth grade at Wadleigh JHS, but in November, following an encounter with a teacher (who claims his wrist and finger were twisted by the 15-year-old), LaQuinn was suspended from regular school for a year.

He is now awaiting placement in an alternative school.

No Books, No Brains, No Chance
JUNE 8, 1994

All over town, people were yelling about the cuts the mayor wants to make in the school budget.

At City Hall, some school superintendents yelled that the cuts were outrageous. In Queens, more than 100 parents yelled that they couldn't stomach the toll on schools in their district.

And at a hearing in an office building across from City Hall, students and alumni of New York's public schools said emphatically that they had come to praise what the schools did for them, not to bury them.

Nobody yelled so eloquently as Dwight David Gregg, who limped into the hearing on the arm of his son, a high school junior. Gregg was in pain because he threw his back out last week, but he couldn't miss this, he said. It was too important.

Gregg is a parole officer who knows the school system through its back end. He sees what happens when people don't get an education. He works in the warrants section of the department, which means his job is to find people who have violated parole, and lock them up. He and his fellow officers go looking for people every day. Sometimes they catch up with two or three, sometimes they get nobody.

The parole-breakers all have one thing in common. They are uneducated.

Gregg first became aware of this when he was a kid growing up in Philadelphia. "In the ninth grade I couldn't read. So I started to act out. I did everything I could to make people miserable. You treat people the way you want to be treated. I didn't like myself, so I treated myself terribly and I treated everyone else terribly." In the 10th grade, he was kicked out of school. He wound up in the Job Corps in Tennessee, trying to learn a trade. Here he found lots of other young men like himself—poor blacks and white hillbillies who, couldn't read.

Gregg later joined the Marines and went to Vietnam. When he looked down the line of soldiers, he saw the same images he had seen in the Job Corps. It was the same folks, guys with little education who couldn't read. Only now they were dying for it. Two years in Vietnam shook him up sufficiently to make him decide to go to college—and graduate—after he came home. He then became a drug counselor, worked in psychiatric hospitals, and finally became a parole officer.

Now when he sees the drug addicts and criminals who file past him, it's like looking at a mirror image of himself as a young man. They have no education, very little self esteem—and like the guys in Vietnam, they, too, are dying.

A few months ago, Gregg was searching for a parole violator who was 22 years old. The fellow had shot five people, and finally somebody shot him. The bullet went through the back of his ear and came out his mouth. But he survived, which made him think he was really bad. When Gregg looked at the shooter's file, what stood out was that he had no education. He had dropped out of school in the ninth or 10th grade.

The guy was finally caught. On the surface he seemed like just a pleasant kid, Gregg said. But he was also ignorant, and he may die for it, too.

"When you have a conversation with these men, you can see they don't know what's really going on in this world. They have no guidance. These are lost folks."

In the jails of this city, only 10 percent of the inmates have finished high school. The state prisons are also pools of ignorance; 75 percent of the inmates have no high school diploma.

Last month, a 17-year-old named Jerome Nisbett was sentenced to 25-years-to-life in prison for shooting a drama teacher in a Brooklyn park. During his trial, the most striking thing about Nisbett was his ignorance, and the feeling that he existed in a moral vacuum. When a police officer read Nisbett's confession in court, it sounded like something a fourth grader would write.

So to Dwight David Gregg, the idea of cutting money for schools is preposterous. In New York City, you have a structure called The Board of Education, but you don't have the funds or the fortitude to see that children get educated. It's a bone with no marrow in it.

Yesterday, people in this city were yelling about the mayor's plan to cut out school antiviolence programs that have names like mediation and conflict resolution. These programs all sound good, but there's no better way to short-circuit a life of crime than by teaching somebody to read.

Analogy Sheds Only Heat
MAY 7, 1990

The slight, balding professor looked nervous.

The lecture hall was full of people waiting to hear him. Some even stood in the aisles. But outside in the hallway, an angry crowd was gathering, and police were standing by just in case there was trouble.

This was my first glimpse of Michael Levin as he appeared at Long Island University last week. Levin is the City College philosophy professor who has been maligned for his racial theories about black inferiority. When he was invited to speak at LIU, some students and faculty objected. But there he was in the lecture hall, while the angry crowd gathered outside. I even thought it was rather brave of him to come and face this audience, many of whom were blacks.

Levin was one of three professors on the panel, which was about urban ethics, and he read his paper first. It was called "White Fear of Crime Is Morally and Epistemologically Justified." I don't have the space to tell you everything he said, but I'll try to summarize his remarks:

1. A recent study concluded that one out of four young black males has spent time in jail or on probation. Black males in urban areas also commit crimes at a much higher rate than white males. So whites are justified in feeling afraid of all blacks.

2. The lightbulb analogy: If you know that one out of 10 Acme lightbulbs is defective, you can't reject the possibility that the Acme lightbulb in your hand might be defective, Levin said.

3. The jogger analogy: While out jogging at night, you [a white person] see a young black man jogging toward you, not wearing a jogging suit. Since there's a 25 percent probability that he is a felon . . . you are entitled to turn on your heels and run the other way.

4. Blackness alone is a sign of danger.

5. Since it's likely that a black man will be a criminal, it's all right for the police to stop and search a black man who's driving a fancy new car. It's also safe to assume that a black man driving a fancy new car is a drug dealer.

6. It's OK to invade the civil rights of some people [blacks] in order to prevent the invasion of other [white] people's rights in the future. So the normal restrictions on search and seizure shouldn't apply to blacks.

7. Affirmative action is bad because it favors blacks and women solely on the basis of their race or sex, without regard to their merits. (However, you shouldn't stop to consider a person's individual merits if he's a black person coming toward you; it's OK to assume that he's a criminal.)

8. White attitudes and prejudice have nothing to do with why blacks commit crimes, and we should stop making excuses for black criminals.

While Levin rattled off the points of his paper, there were snickers and groans from the audience. The questions that followed indicate what the audience thought of his views.

"When you run from the black man in the park, how do you know he's not just out enjoying the park or taking a shortcut to his house?" a black male student asked him.

"Are you telling me that those people were justified in killing Yusuf Hawkins because he was coming to their neighborhood to mug them?" a young woman wanted to know.

"Dr. Levin, I'd like to know how you make it down the street if you're running from everybody who's black?" another young man asked. "How do you get down DeKalb Avenue?"

A young black man with a map of Africa stitched to his jacket asked: "If a black person gets 15 years in jail for stealing a car, what's the penalty for a nation that suppresses a group of people for 130 years?"

Then came the most important question: "What do you hope to accomplish?" a woman asked Levin. "What is your reason for telling these things to students?"

That was the question on my mind as I listened to Levin. He's entitled to his views, to write about them, to teach them, to espouse them in any way he sees fit. This is America. People are free to be bigots and to express bigoted views. If whites are not free to criticize blacks, then blacks certainly can't claim the right to criticize whites—or anyone else, for that matter.

There is a dangerous trend in this country toward stifling any kind of criticism of ethnic groups—blacks in particular. Anyone who dares to suggest that the black community has certain problems it needs to deal with on its own is bitterly criticized.

I happen to think it's important to point out, constantly, that the black crime rate is disproportionately high, that black youths are failing to get an education, that unwed parenthood, drug abuse and crime are rampant within the black community. These problems are partly related to the vicious discrimination blacks have suffered over the years, to their being shut out of the mainstream. But they are also related to some of the failures of the black community itself. If that is Levin's point, then it's worth saying and worth listening to.

The purpose of scholarship, after all, is to make the world a better place. It's one thing if Levin wants to use his statistics on black crime to call for measures to reduce black unemployment, to raise the educational achievement level of black schoolchildren, and reduce racial discrimination—all of which contribute to black disaffection and crime. But that's not his point.

His point is to justify prejudice, to rationalize whites' fears of blacks, not to find ways to rectify a lousy social situation. Dividing people is what he's after, not bringing them together. It's his mean-spiritedness that keeps Levin from being a true scholar, and makes him just a plain old garden-variety bigot.

At one point during last week's panel, one of the other professors was reading his own paper. Suddenly the angry voices in the hall began to grow louder and closer. It seemed that the angry students outside were about to storm the lecture hall.

Suddenly Levin, who had been sitting quietly, jumped up and ran out a side exit. An unceremonious exit for a scholar. But then, I guess the professor who says whites are morally justified in fleeing blacks always has to be ready to flee on a moment's notice.

The Low Road
AUGUST 12, 1991

There's a lot of truth in what Professor Leonard Jeffries has to say. The problem is dealing with the cant that goes with it.

In his now infamous speech, delivered at a black cultural festival, the City University professor posed a simple theory. The education system in the United States, he said, routinely denigrates the achievements of blacks and other minorities, while supporting a system of white dominance.

Education has always been used at least partly as a political tool. Its goal is to socialize people into accepting the values and forms of behavior that society deems acceptable. That the education provided in American schools has historically tended to enforce notions of black inferiority is well-known—at least to the black people who attended those schools.

The bitter opposition to a recent proposal for a multicultural curriculum in New York State schools is only the latest sign of society's refusal to acknowledge that blacks, Asians, Native Americans and Hispanics contributed anything to world history and culture that's worth studying.

So when Leonard Jeffries says his mission is to root out the racism in the educational system and unearth the truth about black people, I applaud him. The problem comes when Jeffries goes from racial uplift to race-baiting. In his speech he talks about going to the movies as a child and being assaulted by the negative images of blacks onscreen: Sambo images, Beulah, Stepin Fetchit.

"It was by design," Jeffries says, singling out the Jewish movie moguls who at that time ran the Hollywood studios. "That was a conspiracy planned and plotted and programmed out of Hollywood, with people called Greenberg and Weisberg and Trigliani and whatnot. I'm not being anti-Semitic to mention who developed Hollywood. Their names are there. MGM . . . Metro-Goldwyn-Mayer. Adolf Zukor. Fox. Russian Jewry had a particular control over the movies. And their financial partners, the Mafia, put together a system of destruction of black people."

Let's analyze this. Were the images of black people that came out of Hollywood in the early decades of the movies degrading? Yes. Were the studios controlled by moguls who were Jewish? Yes. Was there some mob involvement (read Italians) in the movie industry? Probably.

Was there a conspiracy by Jews and Italians to denigrate blacks on film? Probably not in the sense that they got together around a conference table and hatched specific schemes to make black people look bad. But racist attitudes were widely tolerated among white American businessmen.

The movie moguls reflected the bigotry of the country at large and conveyed those attitudes in their movies. In the commercial images of those times, not only were blacks made to look stupid and silly. Italians were portrayed as lowlife criminals. The Irish were painted as thugs and drunks. Jews were depicted as crude and greedy. And American Indians were, well, just in the way.

It is important to know, as Professor Jeffries maintains, that Jewish studio heads played a role in perpetuating such racist images. But to suggest that Jews held a monopoly on denigrating blacks is wrong. The whole American culture conspired to denigrate blacks. Some Jews were just a small part of it.

I gather from his speech that Jeffries doesn't care much for the educational theories of Diane Ravitch. Ravitch writes books about education and happens to be a Jewish woman from Texas. I have no strong views about Ravitch myself, and if Jeffries wants to describe her as the ultimate, supreme, sophisticated, debonair racist, he's entitled to that opinion. But to excoriate her simply for being a sophisticated Texas Jew reveals a demagoguery that undermines him as a scholar.

In his speech Jeffries talks about a study he did recently on the curriculum in New York schools, and about his amazement upon discovering that the section about Africa didn't include anything about the highly advanced civilization of the ancient Egyptians.

"I couldn't believe what I was seeing," Jeffries said, describing the perfidy of the white educators who were trying to rob Africa of its significance in history.

To right the wrongs of this education system, Jeffries already has a big enough job cut out for him. He should leave the race-baiting to others.

Lesson in Survival

JUNE 24, 1991

The public schools I attended in Birmingham, Ala., were, by the strictly objective standards of those times, among the worst in the nation. Alabama spent less money per capita on educating schoolchildren than any other state in the Union, except for Mississippi. Add to that the fact that the schools I attended were racially segregated by law, and that black schools received only about 50 cents for every dollar spent on the already underfunded white schools.

Yet I managed to get a good education from that lopsided school system. It was enough to help get me into a good college and to go from there to graduate school, and to have enough of a career in journalism that people read what I have to say. I attribute the positive impact of those underendowed schools to the fact that they instilled confidence in us. This was the result of having black teachers and principals who not only knew their subject matter, but who also cared about us, wanted us to learn, and knew we were capable. It also had to do with having teachers who knew that the version of history as portrayed in the history textbooks wasn't always accurate.

They knew, for example, that the slaves didn't spend their days singing merrily in the cotton fields, that the cost of taming the American West by the U.S. farmers and the settlers from the east was the decimation of the American Indians, and that the Camelot-like gentility of the antebellum South was really more myth than fact.

Having teachers who could put things in perspective by calling into question the version of history that would otherwise have been fed to us gave us a confidence about our place in history and in the world that we took with us, wherever we went.

College was different. It was a venerable, old institution with high standards, and it offered a sound education. But I found very little there that affirmed who I was. The professors were all white, the writers we read were virtually all white (and practically all male), and most of all, the view of the world was a white one.

According to this view, Europeans and their descendants were the prime movers and shakers throughout the history of civilization. What Europeans did and thought was important. What other groups did and thought was less important, at least not significant enough to be studied. I remember, for example, taking a course in social problems where the three problems we discussed were poverty, crime and blacks.

The impact on those of us students who were black was powerful. This education did not affirm us. It taught us that white culture was relevant and superior, that ours was irrelevant and inferior, and that by inference, so were we.

I thought about the difference between the education I received in those underfunded black schools in the South and in that wealthy white college in the North last week when a New

York State education committee called for changes in the way history and social studies are taught in New York's public schools. The report recommended that teachers give more recognition to the role of nonwhite cultures in the teaching of history.

The report was attacked, even by members of its own committee. Professor Arthur M. Schlesinger, a committee member, for example, rebutted the suggestion that the current teaching about the European colonization of nonwhite countries doesn't address the great loss of lives involved and the destruction of the characteristics of those cultures.

Like infanticide? Schlesinger wrote in his dissent. Slavery? Polygamy? Subjection of women? Suttee? Veil-wearing? Foot-binding?

History, we all know, is written by the victors, by those who won the wars, conquered the territories, and remained in power. It takes on the slant of those who are in charge, usually at the expense of those who are subjugated. Thus, we are taught that Columbus discovered America, even though darker people were living here long before he ever turned up on these shores. Eighteenth-century population maps of the United States portray large portions of the West as uninhabited, as if the Indians who lived there did not exist. And slavery is portrayed as an efficient and relatively benign economic system in which blacks fared better than they would have on their own.

Critics of multicultural education claim that including the views of non-European cultures in the teaching of history is divisive, that it undermines national values, and that ultimately it is unscholarly. But my teachers in Alabama knew better. They knew that history is complex, that there is always more than one version of it, and that including all sides only makes it more accurate. In fact, in the absence of such a culturally diverse approach, what we know as history is often downright incorrect.

Cameras Leave, Learning Resumes

JUNE 15, 1994

"Pick up a book, a pen or a brush, but never a gun" is the slogan painted in bold strokes on the entrance to Springfield Gardens High School.

It is a poignant message for tough times, and it floats above a schoolyard so green and meticulously manicured that I marveled to see it attached to a public school.

Springfield Gardens is an urban high school. It is in New York City. Ninety-five percent of its students are black.

And it has practically everything one could want in a high school:

The great majority of its students are from the middle class. Seventy-five percent of its graduates go to college. The bulletin boards in the halls are lined with the names of seniors who are getting Regents diplomas and students who made the last honor roll.

Yet more than a decade ago, when the Board of Education started letting students attend schools outside their own neighborhoods, Springfield Gardens began losing local kids who looked for schools that were more integrated.

This is a lesson in how a school's reputation can be marred by racial stereotypes, or by sheer bad luck. A few years ago, a New York Post reporter wrote a piece about school violence—and said that, at schools such as Springfield Gardens, students had to walk through a metal detector on their way to class. The school didn't even have a metal detector at the time.

Perceptions often have only a tenuous hold on reality. This week at the school, I heard students talking about their Advanced Placement courses in biology, their Westinghouse Science projects, their summer jobs at Manhattan law firms. They talked about the one day a week they spent studying at Columbia's engineering school and of their acceptances by colleges such as Syracuse, Columbia, Wesleyan and the University of Michigan.

"There've been ups and down, but this school is a wonderful place," said Sharline Saunders, an 18-year-old senior. "If you come here with a positive attitude and want to get something out of it, you will."

"The real strength of the school is the teachers," said Annette Harriott, another 18-year-old senior. "They truly care and want us to succeed."

Nancy Orens was like all the other teachers I met here. She called the students wonderful and fabulous. "I love being in this school," she said. "There is a sense of camaraderie and warmth."

Judy Slotnick, who used to teach in an affluent, white school district on Long Island, has found Springfield Gardens very different.

"At my other school, we used to frisk kids going into the senior prom to make sure they didn't have alcohol. I wouldn't sleep until I heard the kids had all gotten home safely. That is not the case here. When they come to the prom, they handle themselves with such respect and grace. I think they respond to being dressed up.

"By and large, these kids are fabulous. They have such vitality, such life, and they're hungry for success."

The ingredients in this mix are: two-income families who embrace middle-class values; a principal, Pamela Lemelle, who says she is determined to make her school a community of caring; teachers who seem neither cynical nor overwhelmed by school politics, and students who are eager to be shaped.

The school's many good qualities came together last week in the reaction to Micha Chatmon's death in a freak accident at the senior prom. Micha, 17, was killed when a piece of metal fell from the ceiling of the hall where her classmates were having their senior prom. Grief often comes in waves, and Springfield Gardens had its share this school year: a female student was shot in the eye by an outsider on the sidewalk, a beloved assistant principal was burned by acid in an encounter with an agitated student last winter.

When the battalion of reporters stormed in after Micha's death, the people at Springfield Gardens felt set upon by a mob of voyeurs. "The TV cameras were here in seven minutes when one of our students got shot," said teacher Stuart Garfinkel. "Where are they when there's a graduation?"

"These incidents are bad luck, when you look at it," said Edline Jacquet, 18, the senior class valedictorian. "When you look at them from the outside, things look bad, but not if you're here."

"I think it's just the media," said Deno Morgan, 17. "They don't say positive things about the school . . . that's because negative things sell."

When Judy Stern, a guidance counselor, came to the school to do crisis counseling following Micha's death, she thought about all the problems the high school has had recently. "But I was shocked. I saw kids walking through the hallways, literally holding each other up. I saw the cafeteria staff hugging a girl who was nearly catatonic. We get so cynical and see ourselves as burnt-out and uncaring people. But there are things happening in this building that allow people to be connected."

Students at other high schools felt connected, too. The students at Thomas Jefferson High School in Brooklyn, which has had its own misfortunes and has been battered in the press because several of its students have been murdered in recent years, sent a wreath of red roses and white carnations to the students at Springfield Gardens. The card reads "With Sympathy," and the wreath stands in the principal's office.

There is often be a message in a tragedy, and at Springfield Gardens High School, the message is not that life is unfair and that one's efforts are pointless. It is in the fact that students not only were back in school the next day, but that they do their homework, study for their state exams, and have big plans for the future.

Micha Chatmon's death brought reality back to the school— that's the way Stuart Garfinkel sees it. "We've all realized that things could be a lot worse. And we have to remember the good things we do on a daily basis."

Chapter 5

What's up with this? Young and in trouble

A Child Waits for a Knock

DECEMBER 11, 1991

It is known officially as the L train, unofficially as the Canarsie line, but I call it the Train to Hell.

A couple of stops from the end of the Brooklyn leg of this train line, at New Lots Avenue, the refuse of a thousand rotting lives litters the landscape like the vegetation of an alien planet. You see strange things on the streets and vacant lots of Brownsville.

One street is littered for an entire block with the innards of gutted cars. The parts hang from a fence like decorations on a junkman's Christmas tree. Nearby, on a vacant lot strewn with garbage, lies an entire tree trunk, upended, and having lain there so long it has taken on the pallor of petrified wood.

Trees are not the only dead things here. So are the souls and aspirations of many people. Sometimes hope flickers for an instant in the hearts of children, but unless carefully tended, it too becomes as dead as the tree.

Naquina, 13, lives a few blocks from the New Lots subway stop. Or at least you could say she is staying here for a while. For the last two weeks, she has lived in the apartment of her great-aunt in the Nobel Drew Ali housing project. But her great-aunt, who is on welfare and raising four teenage children in four rooms, can't keep Naquina for long.

Before she came to stay with her great-aunt, she lived with a cousin in the same housing project. She stayed there about four months, but left when that apartment got too crowded and nerve-endings frayed.

Before that, Naquina and her mother bounced around for more than a year in homeless shelters. This was after her mother had a falling-out with her boyfriend and the two of them had to move out of his apartment. The first shelter was in Manhattan; the second was in downtown Brooklyn; the third was in the Bronx.

She lived for several years with her godmother in East Flatbush, but says they stopped getting along, so Naquina had to go back to her mother. She has also stayed with her aunts for varying periods, sometimes just long enough to get something to eat and a good night's sleep. Her mother, whom one family friend called a crack addict, lives down the street with a friend and can't provide for her daughter. So Naquina is basically on her own.

"Right now I don't have no place to go," Naquina says. "I guess I'll go to the group home 'cause I don't have anywhere else to go, and I don't want to go back to the shelter. My mother doesn't have enough money to take care of me, and I don't have enough clothes."

She says she has two friends who live in group homes, and they tell her such places are OK. "It be tiring," she said of her wanderings. "I'd like to stay in one place. But there's no place for me to stay except the group home."

It is ironic that to the mind of an unwanted, untended child, moving into a group home—little more than an orphanage, but at least a stable, heated place—can be a lifetime's dream. "I guess a group home would be the best place for her," says Alice Gillman, the great-aunt with whom Naquina is now staying. "If I had the room, she could stay with me. But I've got three boys and a girl. I'm full up."

Gillman is a person perplexed by the difficulties of life. Ask her almost any question, and she shrugs her shoulders with confusion. No, she doesn't know what's wrong with Naquina's mother that she can't care for her daughter. No, she doesn't know how to get Naquina into a residence. And no, she doesn't know what will happen to her great-niece.

Yesterday, the two of them waited in Gillman's cramped apartment, hoping for a visit from the Child Welfare Administration of New York City. The man Naquina calls her stepfather is rearing a 7-year-old son he had by Naquina's mother. He telephoned the CWA this week to report that Naquina is a neglected child. He said he is worried about what will happen to her if she keeps being shuttled around from place to place.

"That whole family is in disarray," he said. "It's a sad, sad situation."

In fact, Naquina has two other aunts in the same building, besides the cousin who lives next door. But in this family, the adults are not minding the store, and the children are on their own.

Last March, Naquina's first cousin, then 12, had a baby in

the same housing project—where she lived with Naquina's mother's aunt and a 21-year-old male cousin. She was impregnated by the young cousin, panicked after the birth and threw the infant down a garbage chute.

That story made headlines. The great-aunt with whom she lived claims she didn't know the girl was pregnant and wasn't home when the child gave birth. The infant lived, the boy cousin was sent to jail and the young girl is now living with a foster family.

In a community where young, untended girls are easy sexual prey, a child like Naquina could easily wind up like her cousin, or even worse off. It doesn't help that Naquina is big for her age, with the body of a 17-year-old and the face and speech of a child.

"Sometimes when I go out, the men passing by in cars call out to me, but I just keep going," she says.

"I'm afraid for her," Gillman says. "She don't have no place to stay. And I don't want her to go out in the streets and do nothing stupid and get hurt."

In her heart, Naquina says, she longs for the days when she was about 7 or 8, when she, her mother and her stepfather had a home of their own. "I want me and my family to get back together." But since her mother's life is in disarray and her stepfather has another family, this seems unlikely.

For now, she and her great-aunt wait in the apartment, hoping for a knock on the door that means someone from a city agency is about to offer Naquina a home. They are just two stops from the end of the L-train line, and about the same distance from a child's ultimate despair.

Black Men Still Have Choices
JANUARY 10, 1990

This week Masai McGrier, a 16-year-old black youth from Harlem, was indicted in the rape and torture of a 12-year-old girl. Even in a city where one grows hardened to heinous crimes, the brutality of this one pricked the sensibilities.

Police say McGrier and two other youths, 14 and 16, abducted the girl and subjected her to hours of torture—including slashing her with a knife, stabbing her with a heated icepick and raping her. Afterward, they dangled her over the roof of an apartment building, but stopped short of dropping her to her death. The youths said they attacked her because she owed them money.

I was struck by the viciousness of the crime, more so because it came on the heels of a lengthy report in this newspaper about the crisis of black men in America. According to the article, black men are in danger of being wiped out by a host of problems, including unemployment, poverty, lack of education, a soaring mortality rate from murder and disease, and the decline of the two-parent family.

It is a familiar litany that has been discussed for years. Social critics, as well as regular folks, tend to talk about the social problems of black communities as a way of explaining why blacks commit such crimes. Blame is given to fatherless homes, dysfunctional families, a lack of recreation facilities, the lack of jobs and the indifference of the schools. I understand from sources familiar with his case that McGrier was raised in a family of drug abusers, that both parents died of AIDS, and that he has a long history of criminal behavior.

I don't dispute the seriousness of the social conditions that seem to trap black men in a destructive vise, but I was disturbed by the article's conclusions. I take issue with its portrayal of black men as helpless victims of society who have no control over the direction of their lives. Black men, like all other groups in society, have choices about what to do with their lives. Because one's options are limited by poverty, family problems, or even racism, does not mean there are no choices.

A few years ago, I was a juror in a murder case in which a black youth was accused of shooting another youth who lived in the same housing project. During the trial, young people from the project testified. I remember feeling that these young adults had potential that could have blossomed if they had received better guidance. There was the young hairdresser who was attractive, but didn't know how to dress properly; the bright young man who had dropped out of high school and didn't speak correct English, and the college student who was struggling to get an education that would take him out of the project. Most had dropped out of high school, and all of them testified about the guns—hundreds of guns—they had seen as young people growing up in the project. I thought that it must be hard to overcome the limitations they faced and to break out of them.

Still, too little is said about the role of choice and moral responsibility in determining the course of one's life. I asked David Hobby, 21, who grew up in Harlem and has seen his share of problems, what he thought about the crisis of black men.

When he was a small boy, David's parents separated and his mother went on welfare. She later got a job as a day-care worker to support her three children. David was kicked out of high school for fighting and spent two weeks in jail for assault. He went through an assortment of jobs—security guard, cashier at Nathan's, stock boy at a supermarket—until he was burned out of his apartment a year ago and found himself homeless. Now he lives at Covenant House, a residence for runaways and homeless young people, where he is studying to be a chef. He hopes to finish the course by this spring, to get a job, and to go back to school for his high school equivalency diploma.

"There's no one crisis for all black men," David told me. "I'm not in a crisis. Everybody has to make their own way in life. The teenagers who raped that girl may go to jail. There are black men out there doing drugs. They are making their own problems.

"Most of my friends from school are in jail or out there selling drugs. I was tempted to sell drugs, but I never did. . . . The turning point for me was when I thought I was going to be homeless and on the streets. I got this opportunity to get my life together."

Does he think black men have some control over their lives? "Yeah, they do. They have choices. They can go out there and study and make their lives something. Or they have the choice to do bad. They let that white stuff put them down."

In my career, which has included interviews with jail inmates, junkies, alcoholics, and troubled juveniles, all have told me the same thing: that the turning point for them was the decision to end the self-destructive behavior. Until then, all entreaties to shape up and all offers of assistance were useless.

I have seen young people living in bleak and depressing conditions. But in almost every case, there were forces that encouraged them to make the right choices: mothers who worked hard and kept immaculate homes, fathers who coached their sons' baseball teams, parents who paid for music lessons and grandmothers who dragged them to church on Sundays. Sometimes it wasn't a relative but a teacher, a social worker, a counselor in some program. The difference between the kids who made it and those who didn't was the decision to accept or reject the help that was offered.

Gordon Lynch, a black man and a counselor at Covenant House, tries to offer help to the young people he sees. "I make them aware of the exploitation that black people have faced. Then I tell them they have to know their own humanity, to know their own worth, and then get out here and do something. They have to force institutions to do something. I tell them, 'Don't tell me you won't go and take a job for $3.25 an hour when you have no job at all.' The fact is, there is a choice between working at a minimum-wage job and selling drugs, and thousands of young people make it every day. And education is not something that is ladled out to passive recipients. It is something that must be aggressively taken."

There are many things that could be done about the crisis of black men. There could be an end to discrimination. There could be more job training, whether sponsored by the government or private business. And there could be more of an effort by black families and black institutions to encourage young black men to make the right choices.

I don't know why the three teenagers accused of rape committed that terrible deed—if, in fact, they are guilty. I do know that whatever problems plagued their private lives, the rape was not inevitable. It was an act of choice, and for this horrific choice there are no excuses.

Another Mindless Crime

JUNE 7, 1993

About the collective dismay that followed the murder of Allyn Winslow in Prospect Park, nobody summed it up better than Mayor David Dinkins.

"Fourteen to 16," the mayor said of the pitifully young ages of the four suspects. "It boggles the mind and crushes the heart to think of it."

First came the horror of the crime: A teacher and father shot dead in broad daylight as he rode his bicycle in the park. Next came its senselessness: The sole apparent motive was to swipe the man's new bike.

For me, there came the usual dread. That feeling is always there when I hear of some new, mindless crime. A kid shot dead in a high school cafeteria. A girl raped and thrown off a roof. A young man stabbed for his sneakers.

With each new atrocity I comb the newspapers for clues about the suspect's ethnic identity, hoping it will be anything other than my own. I pray for Irish names, or names that sound Italian, Hispanic, Jewish, or Asian. Always my fear is that the perpetrator will turn out to be black. And if indeed he is, I think, No, not again, and feel great sadness.

This time my sense of foreboding was justified quickly, since photographs of Jerome Nisbett, Chad Jackson, Robert Brown and Gregory Morris, four black youths from Brooklyn, were carried in every newspaper.

I suspect that when most New Yorkers who are not black hear about a violent crime like the murder of Allyn Winslow, they assume that somebody black did it. The outrage and fear that nonwhites feel about the large percentage of crimes that are committed by blacks makes them expect this. These feelings are rarely articulated in public, but are expressed bitterly in private. "Why do you-all do these things?" they ask. And "Why doesn't the black community put a stop to all the crime?"

Blacks tend to resent this. "What do you mean by you-all?" we snap back. But in our minds we are asking the same question. The arrests of Nisbett, Jackson, Brown and Morris are another occasion for dismay and embarrassment, and cause us to feel not a little anger and sadness.

It's the kind of pain and embarrassment we feel when we're walking down the street and see a black guy thrown up against the trunk of a police car, his hands cuffed behind his back, flanked by two smug police officers. The scene rankles and has a certain poignancy precisely because it is so sad and so familiar.

"What's this about?" we ask ourselves, or in the slang of the neighborhood youths: "What's up with this?"

The litany of crimes never ends. The murder of Allyn Winslow. A cop shot dead in a Newark courthouse last week. And while we know that most blacks will never in their entire lives commit any crime, with each new atrocity we cringe and ask ourselves, "What's up with this?"

Discussions about the causes of black crime are endless too. We blame poverty, racism, the media, rap music, the welfare system, the demise of the family, the Reagan-Bush years. But then you look at the madness of Allyn Winslow's murder and realize there is no way to rationalize this kind of behavior.

Why do four teenagers go into the park thinking it's OK to steal someone else's bike? Why was one of them carrying a gun, for heaven's sake? And who did he get the gun from? And what makes you shoot somebody over a bicycle? What values are being taught to these kids, and by whom?

At Winslow's funeral his relatives and friends mourned him and asked why his death occurred. And over the weekend Philita Jackson, Chad Jackson's mother, cried outside the precinct where her 16-year-old son was being booked for murder.

Meanwhile, the neighbors and friends of the four suspects described them as just normal kids, not at all the type to commit such an awful crime.

"What's up with this?" was the question on everybody's lips.

Why Many Won't Shed Tears Over Flogging

APRIL 4, 1994

At this moment Michael Fay, an 18-year-old from Dayton, Ohio, is sitting in a Singapore jail cell, contemplating the fate of his rear end. A Singapore judge sentenced Fay to six whacks with a rattan cane after he and some other students took part in a wilding spree that involved spray-painting 18 cars and ripping off some public signs.

Fay also got a four-month jail sentence and a $2,230 fine, but it's the caning that has caused an international uproar. Caning is a mandatory punishment in Singapore for many crimes—including vandalism—though it is said to be quite painful and to leave scars. Citizens of Singapore who break the law expect to get whipped, but the idea that this could happen to an American kid has got some folks outraged.

President Bill Clinton, the U.S. ambassador to Singapore, an Ohio congressman, and Michael Fay's parents have denounced this brutal form of punishment and asked the Singapore authorities to spare Michael Fay the rod.

But most ordinary Americans don't seem to agree. The majority of those who wrote to the Singapore authorities and to the congressman took the position: Go ahead and beat the kid.

"If my son had done what this kid did, I'd beat him myself," said a friend of mine, the father of a 19-year-old.

It's not that most of us believe in brutalizing teenagers, but the Michael Fay case strikes a nerve. We are repelled by the arrogance of Americans abroad who think they and their children can disrespect the laws of other countries, and then escape their punishments.

But we are mostly annoyed by the permissiveness of our own country that treats the recklessness of youths as a joke, and doesn't hold them responsible for their misconduct. When another country cracks down on teenage offenders, we like it. We want to see Michael Fay sweating it out in a Singapore jail because we know if he committed the same crime here, nothing would have happened to him.

An 18-year-old, first-time offender in New York City who decided to mess up some cars and got charged with criminal mischief would face no penalty. According to one Department of Probation official, if the kid were white and from a good family, his case would probably be adjourned in contemplation of dismissal. This means if the kid stayed out of trouble for the next six months, the charge would be dismissed and would not go on his record.

If the 18-year-old happened to be a black kid from a less stable family, the official said, he'd probably get probation. Probation is supposed to mean that the kid will get some supervision and guidance, but it really doesn't mean much. The kid might have to report to a probation officer once a month, and if he's got a job he might be required to pay for the damage he caused. That's about it. Basically when kids start getting into trouble, we slap them on the wrist and send them home.

This starts when the kids are really young, say 13 or 14. A young person doesn't get any real attention until he or she has done something really bad. By the time the kid has graduated to serious crimes and is terrorizing our neighborhood, we're ready to send him to jail for a long time.

"There's basically no punishment," Gerald Migliore, director of public information for the New York City Department of Probation, says of the legal system's treatment of kids who are just starting to run afoul of the law.

We've got to send a message to them that the system will take some action, that they cannot do this kind of thing, and we also need to help the kid, because obviously something is wrong.

The Department of Probation is doing this in a limited way through its intensive supervision program for juvenile offenders. Kids who have committed their first offense are required to meet regularly with their probation officers. They are also screened for drug use, and must take tests to assess their educational needs. They may be referred to other agencies for help, if they need it. They're also required to attend half a dozen legal education sessions, where they discuss the law and the consequences of their crimes. However, this is a tiny program that's being tried on a few hundred kids.

A lot of ordinary Americans don't sympathize with Michael Fay's plight because they see their own neighborhoods overrun with fledgling delinquents who are being allowed to mature into full-fledged criminals, without serious measures being taken.

We compare the low level of crime in Singapore to the soaring amount of crime here and the idea of whipping young butts starts to sound good. We don't really want to start flogging 14-year-olds, or 18-year-olds, for that matter. But giving them a few whacks to their psyches at an early age would do us all some good.

Tiny Bird, Pack of Cats
JUNE 18, 1991

She entered the courtroom like a tiny blue bird. Tentative, nervous, her hands sometimes fluttering about her face. She wore a blue dress with a strand of pearls, and looked confused about where to go until a court officer gently guided her to the witness stand. She sat there, at 5-foot-2 and just over 100 pounds, dwarfed by the sprawling courtroom and the spectators who were watching her. She looked more like a teenager than a 22-year-old. Except for the judge, she was the only female in the well of the courtroom. The rest were men in dark suits: the prosecutors, the lawyers, and the three defendants—big, strapping athletes.

The young woman had come to testify in the trial of three of the St. John's University students she accuses of sodomizing her on March 1, 1990: Walter Gabrinowitz, Matthew Grandinetti and Andrew Draghi. The word going around was that she'd be a lousy witness.

Too nervous, not strong enough, they said. Wouldn't go over with the jury.

It's true she wasn't the most impressive witness in the world. Her voice was so soft you could barely hear it. She had to be asked repeatedly to speak up. And she tended to smile nervously at the defendants.

But over the course of several hours, the young woman's story began to emerge. It was a modern-day horror story of how a naive young woman was led on by a man she thought was her friend, how she was lured like a butterfly into a spider web, and was then set upon viciously. It was also a story of why she was susceptible to such abuse, because, like all well-brought-up young women, she was taught to please—and to please men especially.

The young woman testified that she met fellow student Michael Calandrillo at rifle club practice at 6 p.m. that day. Calandrillo will be tried separately. The two were friendly, she said, and their conversation, typical of college students, turned to sexual banter. He asked about her love life and bragged about his sexual exploits. After practice he offered to drive her home, and she accepted. Then, she testified, he excused himself for a moment to make a phone call.

Here is the rest of the story that can be pieced together from her testimony: In the car, he hands her the first line of the evening: He needs money for gas and wants to stop by his house to get some. She agrees. They drive to his house, a student residence known as "Trump Plaza," and he goes inside, leaving her in the car. Then he comes out and hands her the second line: "Come and meet my friends," he says.

She gets out of the car and goes inside, but Calandrillo has disappeared upstairs. I wondered: What were he and his friends talking about in those few minutes?

He returns and invites her upstairs, where she is introduced to Walter Grandinetti and Andrew Draghi, who are eating dinner and watching TV.

Another guy named Tommy comes into the room. The five of them talked, she said, then they invited her to bring some of her friends over sometime to party. The guys began talking about their sexual exploits, and she told Michael she had to go home. The two of them went downstairs. But Michael was called back upstairs, and went.

Again I wondered: What were these guys talking about at that moment?

Calandrillo came back downstairs. Then came the third line: "I have to wait for a phone call. It won't take more than five minutes . . . Why don't you make yourself comfortable . . . I didn't offer you anything to drink." Calandrillo went into the kitchen and returned with some orange drink in a coffee cup, she said. She drank it and it tasted terrible. He told her there was vodka in it. She told him she didn't drink, that drinking made her sick. Then the next line: "It's only vodka. It can't do anything to you."

"I drank it," she said. "I finished it." Calandrillo pressed two more cups of the drink on her, and when she protested he became angry. The next line: "What . . . are you going to make me waste it? What am I supposed to do with it if you don't drink it?"

"I didn't want to upset Michael, so I drank most of the third cup," she said. By this time she had begun to feel dizzy and nauseated. And so began a night of terror that the young woman will never forget. Calandrillo began massaging her shoulders, then undressing her, she said.

"I tried to explain to Michael. I said not now, some other time." She thought about the other guys who were in the house. "I tried to explain I couldn't be seen in someone else's house. I said. 'Michael, I feel real sick.'"

But he continued to undress her, then got on top of her. She passed out. When she came to, she said, "Michael's penis was in my mouth."

From then on, she floated in and out of consciousness. Once, she said, she woke up and found herself naked from the waist up. At one point, she said, Calandrillo was called away, but Walter Gabrinowitz was there, half-dressed, fondling her. When she came to again, Gabrinowitz was sodomizing her, she said, and Draghi stood nearby. "He was choking me," she said of Gabrinowitz, "intentionally. Two other guys were in the room," she said, "just watching.

"I remember I was trying to get up and trying to hold onto Walter to get up. I scratched him. He slapped me." At one point she screamed. "Walter told me, 'You can't scream in here. This is a residential neighborhood!'" While she was in her drunken, dazed state, Draghi and another guy in the room both sodomized her several times, she testified. She screamed "at every-one but Walter," she said, because "he was upset with me."

This was one of the most amazing parts of her testimony. Here she was being cruelly attacked by a gang of men, and she was worrying about disturbing the neighbors and about offending one of her tormentors.

It gets more bizarre. She passed out again, and when she woke up, two of the guys were standing over her wearing Halloween masks. Here is the way she tells it: One of them was Walter. The sexual abuse continued. Gabrinowitz ejaculated in her mouth and ordered her to "drink it!" Two of the other guys ejaculated on her chest.

"I remember I was trying to get up, but Walter was making sure I couldn't get up. Walter was pinning me to the sofa with his hands," she said. He slapped her. Then he told the guys to get dressed and to take her to the Nugget. The Nugget was another residence occupied by St. John's students. They dressed her, carried her to the car, and drove her to the other house, where she said the abuse continued.

At one point, she fell off the sofa onto the floor. She wound up with Gabrinowitz on top of her, she said. "Walter grabbed my foot and my shoes came off and my socks ended up in his hands. He threw the socks in my face. Walter was treating me so awful. He picked me up and threw me back on the floor. He was threatening me. He said I was disturbing the neighbors and making a scene in these people's house."

There may be those who question the woman's story, but I'm not one of them. To me it had the ring of truth. Aside from its picture of brutality and arrogance, two things stood out. First—all the times during the evening when she said Calandrillo slipped away from her, to make a phone call, to confer with his friends? What were they talking about? Were they planning the assault? Plotting ways to lure her into their trap?

The second was about the tendency of women to make an effort to please, to avoid offending anyone, even when the people you're trying not offend are tricking you, abusing you, raping you. Is this why society places so much emphasis on teaching women to be feminine—which translates into pleasing and compliant? Is it so you can then be controlled more easily? The rules seem harmless: Don't offend your host. Don't disturb the neighbors. Be affable.

How amazing, I thought, as I heard this all-too-believable story unfold. How typical. How sad.

A Jury's Wisdom in Scary Suburbs
MARCH 17, 1993

In the Secrets Beauty Salon, hairdresser Daniel Radice was combing a customer's hair when he heard the guilty verdict on television.

"I really thought they were not going to be convicted, you know, because of the way some of the other recent rape cases have come out, like the Kennedy case. But I think they deserved a guilty verdict."

Radice looked animated and pleasantly surprised. But a few chairs away, customer Mary DeLuca was scowling. "I thought they were going to be let off," she said angrily. "I don't think they should have been found guilty. The girl knew what she was doing."

Down the street at the Gourmet Vice Deli, Melinda Hamilton was eating lunch and seemed relieved when I told her what the verdict was. "I think no one thought they would be convicted. I thought there would be so much influence from the community, so much support for them, that they wouldn't be."

But across the street in Willie's Diner, Deborah Pierro said she thought the guilty verdicts were too harsh. "I know the boys. Maybe one or two of them were a little rowdy, but I don't think they deserved this. That girl was really and truly promiscuous. She knew what she was doing."

After a 23-week-long trial and a verdict that was wrenched from the jury as painfully as a newborn from its mother, the residents of Glen Ridge, N.J., are as divided about what took place in the basement of the Scherzer home as they've ever been. The defense had gambled that the jury wouldn't condemn the town's handsome young athletes for engaging in youthful excess with an awkward, retarded girl. But the jury was able to see the nuances of the case more clearly than others.

This was a hard case. Hard to weigh the girl's sexual willingness against the boys' lurid demands. Hard to weigh her sexual precociousness against her emotional vulnerability. In the end, the jurors said, the girl's mental retardation weighed heavily in their decision. It was a powerful verdict, one that said that gross exploitation, even when consented to, is still abuse.

Much has been made of the affluence of Glen Ridge, of how such tattered morality can exist in the midst of privilege. True, there are huge homes and rolling lawns here. But the four young men convicted yesterday were not wealthy, only comfortably middle-class. Still, it is the urban young men who tend to be villified, and whose rootlessness and tendencies toward violence make them highly feared.

But as this case demonstrated, suburbia can be more hedonistic than the city. In the city there are many pitfalls, but little privacy. Parents who fear losing their sons to the urban jungle keep a tight rein on them. In the suburbs there is freedom, the kind that comes from the knowledge that your sons are safe. Boys here are let loose to be boys. In the crush of the city, young men desiring sex are at a loss to find places to have it. So sex is quick and on the run. In Glen Ridge there are big houses, dark basements and plenty of time and privacy to humiliate a needy girl.

The motto was "You get what you can," and nobody told them it isn't right to degrade somebody just because she agreed to it. Not until yesterday, when a jury told them what they did was wrong.

I wonder if the young people of Glen Ridge have learned anything from this trial. What happened in the basement of the Scherzer house took place four years ago, and at Glen Ridge High School, where the four boys, now convicts, were once athletic team captains and heroes, there are no students left who remember them. The case is something the students see in the news, but they don't relate to it much.

When school let out yesterday some female students giggled and scampered away when they were asked what they thought of the verdict. And a male student grinned sheepishly when asked about the case and said, "Frankly, I don't really care!"

I fear that these students might take the lesson of the jury's verdict to be not that it's wrong to do what they did in the Scherzers' basement, but that it's risky because it can get you in trouble.

Even so, one must applaud the wisdom of the jury.

Truth and Consequences
AUGUST 20, 1990

In the end it was one night—and a series of irreversible acts—that caused the undoing of Antron McCray, Yusef Salaam and Raymond Santana.

During their 9½-week trial the three teenagers were portrayed by their parents, lawyers and supporters as the victims of a frame-up and a racist plot. But when they were driven off in a city van to jail they were convicted felons. A hardworking, courageous and agonized jury had examined the facts and seen the truth. The young men were guilty.

It was a sad but just finale to a trial that had set the city on edge. The sadness was in the unanswered question of how all this came to be: how a young woman came to be violated and beaten nearly to death, and how three young men who had never before been in trouble with the law came to do this deed.

In everyone's life there are certain irreversible acts that permanently alter one's future. Resolve or lack of resolve, strength or weakness of character, good judgment or bad lead us to make decisions about which there can later be no turning back. It may be a decision to leave school, to take or not take a job, to resign in frustration, to propose marriage, to admit defeat in divorce, to act under the influence of alcohol or utter words in anger. We may regret our actions later, but we can't alter the consequences of what we've done. The damage is permanent.

And so it was a series of such irreversible acts that caused

Antron, Yusef and Raymond to be in that van the other night. If the support shown for them during the trial was any indication, all three were the objects of concern and caring. Their anguished parents faithfully attended the trial almost every day. We saw pictures of the comfortable apartment building where Yusef and Antron lived. There were neighbors and friends who looked out for them, cared about them, and presumably taught them the difference between right and wrong. But then came the night of April 19, 1989.

"I thought we was going to beat people up and take bicycles and get money," Raymond said in his videotaped confession, describing how that night of outrage began.

A lot has been said about the role that peer pressure played in creating that night of crime. But the fact is that as the violence escalated, there were many opportunities to flee, to have a change of heart. What was the irreversible act for these three teens, the point beyond which there was no turning back? Was it when they first entered the park as a group bent on violence? Was it when they beat up the poor bum and began to feel the blood lust? Was it when they first saw the woman jogger running toward them, or when the first boy grabbed her? Was it when Yusef hit her the first time with a pipe? Or when Antron began to pull her clothes off? Or was it when Raymond began to fondle her breasts?

This is the question that hovered over this case from the beginning. Why, in Central Park that night, did none of them say: "Hey, this could get me in trouble. I've got to get out of here"? And why, as each waited his turn to pummel and rape the jogger, were they not repulsed by the horror of what was going on, enough to say, "Stop, this is wrong"?

After the crimes were committed, there was only denial—by the teens, their parents, and their supporters, who saw racism in the mere fact that the jogger was white and that black teenagers were charged with the crime.

So on Saturday night they took Antron, Raymond and Yusef away in a van. Their parents were devastated, their supporters were angry, and the teens themselves were stunned. Because of all the denial, the frenzy into which the community was whipped by the trial, I suspect the teens view themselves as the wronged ones. Though there is a young woman with a scarred face and body who walks with a limp and who has trouble reading, these young men see themselves as the victims.

But there must be times in the middle of the night, when Antron, Yusef and Raymond are awakened by sudden flashes of the truth, when they realize the true horror of what they did. At such moments they must be forced to remember their own irreversible acts, which ruined their lives and altered a young woman's life permanently.

A Very Unlucky 12-Year-Old Girl
APRIL 20, 1991

It was one of those terribly sad tales: A 12-year-old girl, orphaned at 4, taken in by an apparently neglectful aunt, sexually exploited by an older male cousin in the house. She becomes pregnant, hides it (if in fact she realizes that she's pregnant), gives birth alone, tries to get rid of the baby by throwing it down a garbage chute. The baby is miraculously rescued, and the girl is charged with juvenile delinquency and accused of attempted murder. Meanwhile, the distraught 21-year-old father threatens suicide and is charged with statutory rape.

The story has the squalidness of an urban *Tobacco Road*: a chronicle of a family whose members' lives were out of control. It is about adults whose lives were so screwed up or preoccupied that they totally neglected the young people in their care. The result was a tragedy that had just been waiting to happen.

A colleague of mine observed that most of the men he talked to about this story reacted the same way. They felt relieved that the baby survived. By contrast, the women's initial instinct was to express sympathy for the 12-year-old mother.

When I first heard about the case, I thought of the mother as well, about how frightened, bewildered and lonely she must have been. Negligence at home had clearly led to her being sexually abused. And the fact that no one, not her aunt, her teachers, or any of her neighbors noticed she was pregnant or, if they did, none offered to help her, seemed astonishing to me. I thought of all the changes that took place in her body during the pregnancy and of her inability to understand them; of the pain and terror of giving birth alone in her bedroom, and the desperation that led her to try to get rid of the baby. It's the kind of experience no adult woman, what's more a 12-year-old, should have to endure.

This was a sensational case, but it was only one example of the kind of sexual victimization girls experience every day. Adolescent boys who are troubled and neglected tend to act out their problems by becoming aggressive, committing crimes—taking out their frustrations on others. Adolescent girls, on the other hand, turn their problems inward, often becoming sexual victims. Unprotected by the adults in their lives, lacking self-esteem and struggling to assert their fledgling womanhood, they become sexual prey to the men and boys around them. They are frequently the victims of rape, incest, or of simply being pressured by their peers into having sex at too early an age.

In New York City in 1989, 370 girls under age 15 gave birth to babies, while double that number had abortions. The 12-year-old mother from Brownsville, Brooklyn, may have made the headlines, but she was by no means alone.

"I've seen girls at 11, 12, 13 who were pregnant by their stepfathers, fathers and brothers," says Jeannine Michael, a clinical social worker who runs a Planned Parenthood clinic in the Bronx. "The girls tell you the abuse started when they were 3 or 4. It only comes to light because of the pregnancy."

"I would venture to say that the abuse was there all along," Michael says of the Brownsville mother, noting that the girl's guardian was apparently incompetent and that she lived in the house with three much older boys from whom she was not protected.

"A prepubescent girl is struggling to become separate psychologically from her mother," Michael says. "She takes a step toward heterosexuality, to become her own woman, and she is surrounded by all kinds of boys and men just ready to leap on her. . . . She reaches out to get her affectional needs met with a boy, and she's taken advantage of.

"Add to that the poverty, drugs and emotional deprivation like we have in this case. . . . Her bodily integrity was invaded at such an early age she has no sense of the boundaries of her body. . . . She doesn't know she has the right to say 'leave me alone' because no one has given her this right."

'We as a society are failing these adolescents," says Dr. Ira Sacker, chief of adolescent medicine at Brookdale Hospital, where the Brownsville mother was taken. "Everybody is passing the buck to someone else. The family has the number one responsibility, but it's also the duty of the school, the support groups, the church, the medical profession. Every time you see a child, it's a teachable moment.

"Adolescents want to feel supported and to believe they have a future to look forward to. We've got to help them plan their future and to know that it goes beyond adolescence. Adolescents are going to take risks, and if they don't feel they're going to have a good shot at a future, then all they're going to think about is the moment, and that means taking part in high-risk behavior."

To me the most tragic thing about the Brownsville case is that nobody noticed. The adults in her life simply opted out. Here was a kid, basically alone, having to make it on her own through one of the most traumatic experiences a woman can experience.

In the end, this gross negligence led to a 12-year-old girl's being an orphan, a mother and a delinquent charged with attempted murder—before she even made it to junior high school. And now, officials say, she's bound for foster care—yet another system with no great history of doing well by its children.

No Role Models Here

OCTOBER 11, 1993

In Hempstead, Tex., they are embroiled in a controversy over whether it was right to kick three pregnant girls off the high school cheerleading squad, while allowing a girl who had an abortion to remain.

The story of the Hempstead High cheerleaders pits moralists against feminists, and in the debate the issues have gotten as muddled as they always do when sex and activism share the same stage.

Three issues seem to dominate this discussion:

1. Are you encouraging abortion when you let a girl who chose abortion stay on the squad, while kicking off those who chose to keep their babies?

2. Is it sexual discrimination to punish the pregnant girls while not also punishing the fathers?

3. Can a pregnant teenager still be a role model, and is she any less a role model than a girl who aborted her child? The first two issues don't concern me nearly as much as the third. Because I believe in a girl's right to choose an abortion and consider it a reasonable alternative to an unwanted pregnancy, I'm not concerned about society's encouraging her to choose that route, rather than ruin her young life.

And yes, if a school is going to "punish" girls who become pregnant, then they ought to punish the fathers as well. What disturbs me is the silly debate over role models and whether a pregnant teenager is a good one. She isn't, and I see nothing wrong with a school's setting standards that say teenage pregnancy is bad. I have no problem with kicking a pregnant teen off the cheerleading squad and no problem with kicking the father of her child off the football team, either.

We have learned that despite our speeches and protestations, we can't keep teenagers who want to from having sex. What we can do is encourage them to take precautions and let them know that irresponsible and unprotected sex is the real height of immorality.

In this country, one-fourth of all girls will become pregnant by age 18, and more than 1 million teenagers become pregnant each year. The United States has a teenage pregnancy rate twice as high as England, France and Canada, three times as high as sexually "free" Sweden and seven times as high as the Netherlands.

I can find little to recommend pregnancy to teenagers, not because it might interfere with their careers on the cheerleading squad or the football team, but because it disrupts their whole lives. Girls who become teenage mothers are more likely to wind up being less-educated adults, poorer, with more children and more kids outside of marriage than women who wait until their 20s or later to become mothers. Many males don't want the burden of another man's children, so teenage mothers are often doomed to a future of unpromising and uncommitted relationships that result in more children that they will have to raise by themselves.

Teenage mothers are more likely to be dependent on public assistance than other women. And the future toll on their children is likely to be great—lower intellectual and academic achievement and more behavior problems. The daughters of these teen mothers are also more likely to become teenage parents themselves.

There are many reasons for the teenage pregnancy epidemic, not the least being our squeamishness in dealing with teenagers' sexuality. We are quick to moralize about the wrongness of teenage sex and then hide from the fact that it's going on all around us. We evade discussions about birth control, shy away from urging effective methods on sexually precocious teens out of political correctness and racial paranoia. We equivocate on abortion.

In the end, it's not the fact of having sex, but the consequences of irresponsible and unprotected sex, that disrupts teenagers' lives. Yet we refuse to take practical steps to address a real problem.

We need to move into the 20th century on these issues. But that doesn't mean that our schools shouldn't say what kind of behavior they think is good and ought to be emulated and what is bad and ought to be discouraged. Students need to know what kind of conduct is likely to pull them down.

Football players and cheerleaders are certainly role models for other students, though they tend to be models of what it means to be popular and attractive, cool and cute, more than anything else. Scholars and student council presidents, heads of drama clubs and editors of student newspapers are role models of a different kind, and their skills are better examples of what it takes to succeed in the adult world.

Cheerleaders aren't generally regarded as models of chaste

femininity anyway, and in recent decades they've been viewed more as high school sex symbols than paragons of virtue.

Barring someone who's involved in a pregnancy from being a cheerleader or a football player or a student council president is a way of saying, no, we don't encourage students to make this choice for their lives.

A teenage mother or father is not a role model, no matter how you slice it. There is nothing wrong with a school, a school board or anyone else saying so.

Some Parents Don't Deserve Children

MAY 24, 1993

He was 4 years old, with bright brown eyes, and like all children was born with endless possibility. In the end he was reduced to garbage, a tiny soul with the life beaten and strangled out of him, wrapped in plastic in a trash compactor, discarded with the rest of the day's leavings.

It was bad enough that Kayesean Blackledge's life ended so prematurely. But the final insult was that he was thrown away, discarded like trash. This was the metaphor that made his death so bitter. Kayesean was a symbol of all the children who are abused, who have the life squeezed out of them physically or emotionally, and then are dumped onto the garbage heap.

They are children with value who nonetheless wind up in trash compactors. They are disposable children, and their stories gall. Why not keep the children, and put their parents out with the trash?

Yesterday police searched for the meaning of the incident that left Kayesean's adoptive mother in the hospital and the boy lying among rotting food. But his story was clearly one of those heartbreaking tales of a child who was neither planned nor wanted, and so was passed on and abused.

He was born to a mother who was only 15, who gave him up to a situation that seemed bizarre. That's not to say you can't be a good adoptive parent if you're transsexual or transvestite, but Kayesean's seemed like an unstable existence.

Stories like that are multiplying, and after a while their onslaught causes more numbness than pain. Two babies were abandoned in February, one a newborn left in a gym bag in a frigid park, the other a baby only a few weeks old thrown into a trash bin.

A severely handicapped 9-year-old boy in a wheelchair is abandoned by his father at a Long Island bowling alley, the father exhausted with trying to care for him. And over the weekend a woman knocks on an apartment door in the Bronx, asks the man who lives there to hold her baby, then leaves and does not return.

A city councilman sires eight children by four different women and barely supports any of them. So the children are left here and there while he flees inquiries about whether he's even entitled to be on the City Council, since apparently he doesn't live in the district he represents.

Such behavior gives the lie to our protestations that we love children. We have proclaimed a day, a year, even a "decade of the child," yet everywhere we look children are being disposed of, thrown out with the garbage.

People can recite a litany of stresses that drive parents to abandon their children. Too-young girls who are freaked out, panicked. Women without resources who nonetheless have one baby after another and must support them on the public dole. Drug addicts who conceive children in between highs and then dump them in hospitals or with relatives. Women who know they are HIV-positive but get pregnant anyway and choose to bear the children, running the risk of passing along the virus and certain death to their children.

And yet we are sympathetic to these parents. We do not wish to hold them responsible. We cringe at the idea of putting restraints on reproduction, even giving birth control implants to teenage girls. We say people have a constitutional right to bear children. We say parents' rights must be respected. So under the theory that it is best to keep families together, we give abusive parents too many chances, meanwhile holding children's lives in limbo, so the parents can "get themselves together."

The fact is there are just too many people who should never

have children in the first place, and when they do, they ought not be allowed to keep them.

The children know this. We send out the message that we love children, but they are not fooled. You could see it in the wide, frightened eyes of the children in the Linden Houses, where Kayesean's body was found, and you could hear it in the voices of the children near his home in Jersey City, N.J.. It was a question: Are we worth so little? And will this happen to me, to be discarded, disposed of, like yesterday's scraps?

I say if it comes to that, throw the parents out with the trash and keep the children.

Tell Success Stories, Too

APRIL 12, 1993

The New York Times has been running a series of articles lately about children in the inner cities. With great sensitivity, the profiles describe how these children and teenagers are coping with the forces that threaten to destroy their lives.

Most of the profiles have been about black children, and I especially liked them because they showed that these kids are not just passive victims of these forces, but are actively struggling against them. The media usually paints pictures of black children who have already lost the struggle. We read about youths who have committed crimes, young people who have surrendered to drugs, and girls who are caught in the mire of premature motherhood and welfare subsistence. So it's heartening to read about black kids who are trying to avoid that fate.

There's still another story about black kids that hardly ever gets told, however. It's about black kids whose parents are doing their job—going to work every day, setting a good example for their kids, teaching them good values, setting rules, imposing discipline and preaching the value of education.

It's the story of children who are smart, creative, sensitive and ambitious, who don't engage in antisocial behavior, and who have goals they are working toward in a logical way. In fact, these traits describe the black kids I know personally far more accurately than all the negative stories we've grown used to.

In this country blacks as a group are portrayed as being mired in toil and trouble and constantly fighting major demons. In fact, most of the black people I know lead pretty standard lives. Consider this: While blacks are widely perceived as being poor and in need of public aid, two-thirds of all blacks in this country are not poor. They happen to work, pay taxes and provide a decent standard of living for their children.

While the popular image of the welfare mother is that of a black woman, in fact the number of black mothers and children on welfare is approximately the same as the number of white mothers and children on welfare. And while the typical image of young black men and women is of people who are undereducated and underemployed, more than 60,000 blacks graduate from college each year.

When I think of the black youths I know, the word "hoodlum" never comes to mind. Instead, I think about boys like A, who lives in my building and who I've known since he was 4 years old. At 18, he is smart, musically gifted, a respectful son and a gentleman. As far as I can tell, he's never seen a gun or done dope, and my image of him is not of him hanging out on the corner, but of him walking another neighbor's dog. He was raised by a single mother, a nurse, and is one of the best examples of successful child-rearing I've ever seen.

When I think of black girls, I think of kids like M, whose parents, both professionals, are paying a considerable sum to keep her in private school. An 11th-grader, she wants to be a journalist, and since we met a few months ago she has pursued me with the relentlessness of an adult, plying me with questions about what it's like being a journalist and what she needs to do to become one.

When I think of the black parents I know, I don't think of crack-addicted mothers or runaway fathers. I think of J, a single woman and a talented journalist who adopted her now-18-year-old son when he was 4 years old. A fair chunk of her salary goes to pay for his private school, and a lot of her energy goes into helping him find summer jobs and seeing that he's exposed to good adult male role models.

I also think about L, a divorced father of two sons who live in another state, who worries about his children constantly, and lately has been spending a lot of time on the phone talking with his older son about his plans for college. I also think about a black woman I met a few years ago. We happened to be discussing pianos, and she told me about having to sell her cherished piano to help pay for her son's medical school tuition, a gesture she didn't seem to regret.

Middle-class blacks are often made to feel ashamed of their accomplishments, to feel guilty about having things when other blacks have less. And we in the media seem to feel that if we acknowledge that most blacks in this country are holding their own and are not a burden to anybody, then we are somehow abandoning the blacks who are in trouble and need help.

The fact is most of the black kids I know don't use drugs and wouldn't think of ripping somebody off, and the kinds of street values that are often imputed to them are as foreign to them as the prospect of their enjoying country-western music. We should tell their stories too. To do so wouldn't deny the struggles of those black kids who are having a more difficult time. It would only paint a more accurate picture.

Chapter 6

Why are the heroes always white?

Grading on the Curve

OCTOBER 24, 1994

"It's a white lady!" somebody whispered, and a hush would fall over the room of black schoolchildren in Birmingham, Ala.

Our class was being paid a visit by one of the white public school supervisors (there were no black ones), and such occasions always filled us with awe. For the few moments that the white lady was in our classroom, all talk and activity ceased.

Our fascination with her resulted from a rigid system of segregation that allowed us only the most minimal contact with white people and that told us in so many ways that they were superior to us. For example, we always called a black female, like our teacher, a black woman, while a white female was always referred to as a white lady.

Our parents and the other adults we knew told us we were as smart as white people and that we could be successful in life if we worked hard and got an education. But it is a long trip from being told something to believing it. So it came as a surprise to me when I came north to a white women's college and discovered that white people were not as smart as I had been led to believe. Blacks often have this revelation when they are exposed to whites for the first time.

Now, there is a new book out called *The Bell Curve,* which is driving people crazy because its authors claim they have evidence that black people as a group are naturally less intelligent than whites. We hear this every 10 years or so, but in their book, Charles Murray and Richard Herrnstein offer study after study and chart after chart showing that, other things being equal, American blacks as a group have an average IQ that is 15 points lower than American whites as a group. The authors give us statistics showing that low IQ is related to all kinds of social ills—including crime, poverty, out-of-wedlock parenthood, welfare dependency, unemployment, and a high dropout rate.

Blacks as a group suffer disproportionately from these problems, the authors say, because they are simply less smart. Of course there are blacks with very high IQs and whites with very low IQs, but there are proportionately fewer smart blacks in the black population than there are smart whites in the white population, the book says.

The most serious theory in the book is that while individual blacks can break out of the mold—by being more intelligent than the norm and/or by being successful despite being less smart, blacks as a group can't rise from the bottom of society. That's because their fate is tied to their intelligence and their lower intelligence is a hereditary thing.

The Bell Curve has caught fire because it states the quietly held belief of many people. The belief that blacks are, by nature, intellectually inferior to whites is the reason well-meaning whites can call for equal opportunity, but flee in horror at the prospect of blacks moving into their neighborhoods or the possibility of their children going to school with black children.

And quiet as it's kept, there is the burning fear in many blacks themselves—like us children in that classroom—that this might be true.

Murray and Herrnstein make their argument for black intellectual inferiority so smoothly, and with such professions of goodwill, that they are difficult for nonscholars to attack.

They say that current social programs aimed at lifting the disadvantaged—welfare and special-educational programs for disadvantaged children—are a waste of time and money. Such programs can't help the underclass, they argue, because the real reason they're at the bottom of the heap is that they are not very smart, and this is largely because of their genes.

Those scholars who believe that all kinds of things contribute to intelligence and hence to success—like home environment, the quality of schools and racism—are attacking the book as dangerous and a tool of the conservative agenda. The argument over how heredity versus environment affects intelligence will never end.

But consider this. Suppose it is true that there is a difference in IQ between blacks as a group and whites as a group, and that this difference is at least partly explained by heredity. One might be able to make a case that the Irish affinity for heavy drinking is in their blood and that Asians have an innate talent for music and mathematics.

That there may be some truth in it does not mean it has to control their destiny.

We know from experience that what makes a person successful in life has as much to do with personality, drive, luck and one's advantages as it does with how smart they are. Madonna and Reggie Jackson have higher IQs than former president John F. Kennedy.

Of those black schoolchildren who were awed by a white woman in those Jim Crow classrooms in Birmingham, I can name at least one university president, a TV producer, a federal judge, an international banker and numerous doctors, lawyers, professors and successful actors and musicians.

The wonder is not that so many blacks in this country remain mired in difficulties. The miracle is that given whatever handicaps they have faced, so many have beaten the odds.

Useful Scapegoats
JUNE 28, 1993

If you believed the rhetoric and reportage of recent days, the Holy War is swooping down on America like a hurricane.

If you didn't realize this when a ragtag band of religious fanatics blasted a hole in the World Trade Center last February, then it should have become clear last week when the FBI arrested Siddig Ibrahim Siddig Ali and his alleged fellow conspirators as they stirred up their now infamous witches' brew.

Once again photographs of Sheik Omar Abdul Rahman appeared everywhere, as law enforcement officials, journalists, terrorism experts and politicians tried to link him to the bombing plot. It is Them against Us, the headlines screamed, although it was not entirely clear who them and us are supposed to be.

The bombing of the World Trade Center was tragically real. So, it appears, was this latest foiled bomb plot. But it is dangerous to create sweeping scenarios of holy wars and international terrorist conspiracies. There is no evidence that either of the plots was part of a highly organized plan, that they were supported by any government, or that they were anything more than the dangerous work of amateurish, low-level radicals.

But such incidents, embellished by the press and latched onto by those for whom terrorist conspiracies serve political and economic purposes, can result in paranoid and reactionary behavior. With the Evil Empire dead and the Cold War, which consumed so much of our energies for so long, fizzled out, are we in need of a new archenemy to fill the void? Nations, especially those feeling newly vulnerable, often for economic reasons, frequently find unity within by having a monstrous alien enemy.

The existence of such foes supports a lot of political functions—a strong military, a beefed-up national security intelligence apparatus, a crackdown on immigration. They also serve the psychological function of bringing the people of a nation together and promoting patriotism.

State Department statistics have shown no increase in terrorist violence in recent years. In fact, the figures show a decline in such activity. But the United States, which until recently has enjoyed the comfort of being insulated from the troubles of the rest of the world, is beginning to see some incidents here. We feel more vulnerable, and we contrive wide-ranging plots.

Professor Richard Bulliet of Columbia University's Middle East Institute believes there has always been a xenophobic current in American life that becomes apparent from time to time, partly because we are so distant from other parts of the world. This xenophobia is accompanied by fears of conspiracies and the targets of that fear are often poor immigrants, who don't in themselves have the apparent ability to threaten the society, and who therefore must be part of a broader conspiracy.

Americans eat this up, Bulliet says, especially when the xenophobia is directed at poor and mysterious immigrants with exotic languages and religions.

"This was a real conspiracy," Bulliet says. "But there were bombs thrown by anarchists in the past. I don't want to minimize the danger of violent groups or underappreciate the skill and ability of the FBI and the police to uncover these groups. What I deplore is the yen to discover a broader conspiracy than is demonstrated in the available information.

"For example," Bulliet says, "when an abortion clinic is bombed, no one blames the Catholic priest who preached a sermon against abortion. Yet since the World Trade Center bombing, the hunt to implicate Sheik Rahman has been on."

Violent acts by Islamic fundamentalists who feel their countries have been corrupted by modern secularism and who want to return to pure Islamic states have been occurring for a while now. The practitioners believe the biggest corrupting influence has been the United States, which has supported the regime of Hosni Mubarak in Egypt and propped up the state of Israel.

These feelings and the terrorist acts inspired by them are not new, but Americans have so little knowledge of other cultures that when these events happen here, we are blindsided by them. Suddenly we see a worldwide conspiracy against us.

The danger of all this is a response that is reactionary. Last week local politicians were calling for Rahman's arrest. The sheik is already deportable anyway because of breaches in immigration law. We don't have to violate the Constitution by straining to connect him to a bombing plot.

There have also been calls for a crackdown against Islamic fundamentalists seeking to enter this country. And attacks on members of the Muslim community multiplied after the World Trade Center bombing.

All this is dangerous. Many of the alleged dangers of the Soviet Union were invented during the long years of the Cold War and were sustained for political and other self-serving reasons. We shouldn't do the same thing with the great Islamic Holy War against America.

The Color of Heroism
DECEMBER 6, 1989

Why are the heroes always white?

The question hit me as a TV commercial flashed across the screen the other day. Here was a promo for an NBC movie about the Howard Beach case, the notorious incident in which white youths beat three black men and chased one to his death in Queens. And again, the hero of the drama was a white man.

The movie focused on Charles Hynes, the special prosecutor in the murder trial. "Only one man can unravel the mystery and bring the guilty to justice," the announcer intoned, as the camera pushed in on actor Daniel Travanti's sensitive face. I got that old, uneasy feeling—a sinking sensation, then disbelief, then anger.

And then the question: Why are the heroes always white?

It's a question that has dogged me for years, as I've watched TV and movie portrayals of historical events involving blacks and whites. Often the real heroes and heroines were black. They were people who stood up to mobs, led unpopular movements, were fired from their jobs, went to jail, were beaten and killed, argued cases in court, and masterminded brilliant strategies for change. But in the movies and on TV, the heroes were always white.

I felt this way when I went to see the movie *Cry Freedom* some months ago. The movie purports to be about the relationship between Steve Biko, the South African freedom fighter who led the black consciousness movement there, and Donald Woods, the white journalist who wrote Biko's biography.

In the movie, Biko, played by Denzel Washington, was an icon, a saint who existed primarily to raise Woods' consciousness about racial injustice in his country. Biko died halfway through the film, leaving me to watch Woods' heroic efforts to smuggle his book out of the country—which took more than an hour. I saw Woods' struggles with conscience, the hardships inflicted on his family, his heroic dash across the border, actions that underlined his nobility.

I watched and thought: If Biko led the movement, underwent the torture and died for his beliefs, becoming a hero for a whole generation of South Africans, why was Woods the hero of the movie? Why not a story that began with Biko's childhood in the Soweto slums and showed how he became a freedom fighter? What about his struggles with conscience, his role as a father and husband, his courage—in short, his humanity?

Things didn't get better in the new movie A *Dry White Season,* also about racial injustice in South Africa. A white schoolmaster, played with haunted intensity by Donald Sutherland, learns about racial injustice in his country through the dire events that befall the son of his black servant.

Black actor Zakes Mokae, playing a revolutionary, instructs Sutherland on the realities of black life. He is compelling, but exists primarily to enlighten Sutherland, the white liberal. It is Sutherland who stares down the scorn of his white friends, who loses his job and his family over his beliefs. And it is Sutherland who is clearly the hero. The other hero is Marlon Brando, as a crafty, cynical civil rights lawyer.

Euzhan Palcy, the black director of A *Dry White Season,* said she had to show the interactions of both blacks and whites in order to portray South Africa accurately. The truth is that once MGM/United Artists took over production, it became a white film—and in that perspective, blacks cannot be the main heroes.

The reason for this is that white movie and TV producers, like many others of their color, find it difficult, if not impossible, to ascribe nobility to another race. Being a hero requires intelligence, courage, and moral conviction, which to many whites are essentially white traits. Blacks can provide emotion, inspiration, even be martyrs to a cause. But whites must be the main movers and shakers. Their reluctance to recognize blacks as heroes is essentially a failure to recognize their humanity.

Take *Mississippi Burning,* a recent hit movie about the civil rights struggle in the South. The movie's moral stance makes it genuinely affecting, but while it claims to document the biggest black revolution in recent history, it contains not a single major black character, and its hero is a white FBI agent. Earlier this year there was a TV movie about former Alabama attorney general Richmond Flowers. Flowers was portrayed as a courageous man who risked public condemnation and imprisonment in his battle to subdue the Ku Klux Klan.

I lived through the civil rights struggle in Alabama, and I know who the real heroes were. As a black child I barely heard of Richmond Flowers. At best I knew he was a white moderate who was doing his job. I did know about people like Arthur Shores, the black NAACP attorney whose house was bombed so many times that his neighborhood was called Dynamite

Hill. I knew men and women who turned out for mass meetings when the movement came to town, at the risk of losing their jobs. I knew schoolchildren who faced Bull Connor's police dogs and fire hoses, and even went to jail.

I knew the black ministers and business people who crafted the marches, boycotts and other strategies that brought down segregation in the South, and did it with skill, and at great personal risk.

Watching the Howard Beach movie the other night, I saw Daniel Travanti's earnest face. I saw Hynes portrayed as a loving husband, concerned father and conscientious citizen; saw his attractive, socially conscious children; his cool persistence in the trial. But Hynes was a public servant doing his job. He was not the hero of this piece.

The real heroes were C. Vernon Mason and Alton Maddox, the feisty lawyers who led the marches protesting the Howard Beach killings. They forced the issue of white-on-black violence into the public eye. By withholding the cooperation of key witnesses, they forced the appointment of a special prosecutor. They were criticized by blacks as well as whites, but they were right. Their subsequent unethical conduct in the Tawana Brawley affair brought them well-deserved ignominy, but doesn't detract from the fact that they were the heroes of Howard Beach—along with thousands of other black (and white) heroes who marched there and in Manhattan to say that black life in this city would no longer be counted cheaply.

Blacks are assigned starring roles in many dramas. We are in the spotlight when it comes to crime and drugs, the welfare quagmire and the decline of the public schools, the crisis of unwed parenthood, and a thousand other pathologies of our times. Some of the negative attention heaped on us is warranted, some not. But we deserve to get top billing when we fit that role, and to be the heroes in our own stories.

When Boycotts Were for Just Causes

FEBRUARY 4, 1991

One of the sorriest chapters in New York City's recent history drew to a close last week when a Brooklyn jury acquitted Pong Ok Jang of slapping Jiselaine Felissaint.

Jang is the assistant manager of the Family Red Apple store, which is still being boycotted more than a year after Felissaint, a Haitian-American, accused Jang of slapping her during a dispute over an attempted purchase.

The boycott became a lightning rod for racial tensions in the city. Its leaders used the alleged assault as a symbol of the disrespect they said is shown to black patrons by Asian merchants in black communities. Its critics viewed the boycott as a simple case of race-baiting.

Last week a jury revealed Felissaint for what she is: a phony, an opportunist and a liar; a woman who fabricated a racial incident to fuel a civil lawsuit against the store. And it showed the boycott's supporters for what they are: people who are willing to use lies to promote a cause, who raised the cry of racism in the absence of a bona fide injustice, and who did a great disservice to the many legitimate black claims for justice.

As a child growing up in the South, I saw the boycott used many times for just causes. In Birmingham, Ala., we boycotted department stores to protest the fact that blacks could not work there or eat at lunch counters. The modern civil rights movement was born with a boycott—when blacks, angered by Rosa Parks' arrest for simply sitting down in a white seat on a bus, refused to ride the buses until blacks were treated equally. What could be more American than using economic clout to protest oppression? These boycotts were just, and they were effective.

When I first learned about the Family Red Apple boycott, I too thought it was just. A black woman had been abused and insulted, so I heard, and this apparently was part of a regular pattern of this store's abuse of black customers. So the community was showing its disapproval by not shopping there.

However, the Flatbush boycott quickly became something

perverse. The protesters rejected all attempts by the store owner to extend an olive branch, to apologize for any injustice that may have occurred or was perceived to have occurred, to try to talk sense.

Then along came Sonny Carson and his band of thugs, who further resisted all attempts at reconciliation. Their angry words were soon being leveled at all Asian merchants who, they said, came into the black community and opened stores when black people couldn't. They didn't want to settle the dispute. They wanted to drive Family Red Apple out of business. They didn't want peace. They wanted to keep the anger going.

As the boycott polarized the city, Mayor David Dinkins wimped out. At first his staff tried to mediate the dispute, but they too encountered the intransigence of the boycotters. As months went by and the boycotters revealed themselves as demagogues, the mayor stayed away from the dispute, afraid to denounce the boycott for fear of alienating his black supporters.

It took Fred McCray, a shy Brooklyn high school teacher, and a group of his students to say that the boycott had gone on long enough—by going to the store and making purchases. The mayor followed suit a few months later.

One of the saddest things about the boycott is that it cheapened the many legitimate protests of black people. Sometimes you realize that some people don't want real progress. They just want to be angry. In this case, they took a bogus incident and exploited it, claiming to create an issue when there was none.

Like all demagogues, the boycotters operated on the assumption that the only way to unite black people is to keep them angry and that the way to keep them angry is to convince them they are perpetually being victimized. They feared that if they let go of the victim routine, they'd have no unity, no cause, and, worst of all, nothing to do.

The real shame is that something constructive could have come out of the Family Red Apple affair. The protesters could have used it as an opportunity to sit down with Asian merchants and voice their concerns about the treatment of black patrons and the hiring of blacks in Asian stores. Since they complain that there are no black-owned grocery stores in the area, they could have used the incident as impetus to raise capital and open one, perhaps the first of many.

But that would have been too much work, would have taken too much time, would have required a real commitment instead of just angry words. This sad pattern of thinking was further reinforced after the jury's verdict last week. Within hours after Jiselaine Felissaint was exposed as a liar, the boycotters returned to the store, intent, they said, on shutting it down. And for what?

Meanwhile, Felissaint threatened to return to Haiti—since, she said, she could get no justice in this country. Good riddance.

Past Embers Fuel Today's Rage
SEPTEMBER 21, 1992

At the Slave Theater in Brooklyn the other night, Al Sharpton was welcomed as a conquering hero.

The several hundred who gathered here were all his people, and the night before had been his victory night. He had trounced Liz Holtzman and come in third behind Robert Abrams and Geraldine Ferraro in a U.S. Senate primary race where he'd been labeled a shoo-in for last place. So when he entered the hall they stood up and crowned him with their applause.

Every Wednesday night the United African Movement holds a meeting at The Slave Theater. It is part community meeting and part nation-building session, part educational forum and part rally. Sharpton and Alton Maddox preside here, and invited guests speak about issues of concern to those who attend.

On this night a panel of journalists was discussing the election results. The talk was upbeat. The election had reaffirmed the changing face of ethnic politics in New York City. Two black congressmen had fended off serious challenges to their seats. A Hispanic woman had routed a longtime, white male congressman. And Sharpton had proved to the world that he was more than just the leader of a ragtag, fringe group of 200 or so.

Sharpton's entrance brought the panel discussion to a halt. Tired and hoarse, he held forth briefly about all the battles he, Maddox and some of those in the audience had been through together. He threw out names like Howard Beach, Bensonhurst, and the Days of Outrage demonstrations. The crowd roared.

Then Sharpton left and the panel discussion continued with questions from the audience. To be a member of the black-owned press at one of these gatherings is to be welcomed as an ally. To be a black employee of a white newspaper is to be a sitting duck. The question, asked by an angry man, was directed at me:

"How can you sit there and say . . . after all the years that black women have been oppressed by white men . . . after all the injustices that the criminal justice system has perpetrated on black people . . . after the ridiculous statements by the white media that Tawana Brawley smeared excrement on her own body . . . how can you sit there and say that Tawana Brawley lied?"

Nobody had mentioned Tawana Brawley until then, but the question was inevitable. For if Sharpton and Maddox are the high priests at The Slave on Wednesday nights, Tawana Brawley is the high priestess. Brawley has long since moved out of the state, acquired a Muslim name, and she has long since abandoned the world of celebrity for the quieter pastures of the college student. Even Sharpton these days shrugs off questions about the Brawley affair when he's in racially mixed company. "You may choose to disbelieve her, but I choose to believe her," he says.

But on Wednesday nights at The Slave Theater, Tawana Brawley's ghost haunts the hall, and those who come here still seek affirmation from outsiders that what Tawana said about being raped by a group of white men was true. There are those who believe you're not on the side of black people unless, in every instance where blacks and whites are in conflict, you agree that the blacks are right.

"I'm not going to debate the Tawana Brawley case with

you," I told the man. "You may choose to believe her, but I happen not to believe her."

An angrier, more abusive man tells me: "You write for the white press and you just write whatever they tell you! . . . But there's only one way of thinking . . . and that's to think black!"

On the morning of the same day as the meeting at The Slave Theater, 10,000 cops who were thinking "white" converged on City Hall. They drew demeaning pictures of the black mayor and made racial slurs at a black city councilwoman. It was a white-power rally aimed at criminals who are often dark-skinned, and at a black mayor who was trying to make cops accountable when they behave like thugs. It was a scene of extreme ugliness.

The people who gathered at The Slave Theater that evening had witnessed this scene. They also knew about all the alarms that have gone off in their community in the past, emergencies to which no one responded. So on this night they celebrated the political victory of one of their own, and kept alive the memory of a ghost who tripped a false alarm.

His Brother's Keeper

MAY 4, 1992

He was a black man who saw an Asian man who'd been beaten nearly to death by a furious mob. Greg Williams, risking injury and the possibility of his own death, went to the man, lifted him off the ground, and walked him to safety. Hence, a human being escaped the list of the dead in Los Angeles.

It was one in a seemingly endless series of vignettes from four days that brought out the best and the worst in people, and the result is a scrapbook of violence and hatred, courage and humanity that is seared into the nation's consciousness.

The incidents in Simi Valley and Los Angeles last week laid out in stark relief the scenario of race relations in this country. We talk about harmony and understanding, but then we see pictures like those, up close and in our face.

First the jury verdict condoned beating a man in a way no

one would condone beating an animal. The verdict came from a not very intelligent jury, and affirmed the idea that blacks are inferior, animal-like, dangerous, and therefore can be treated as less than human. The belief in black inferiority has always been the essence of racism, and there it was, spelled out in capital letters.

Then came the scenes of people looting stores and beating and killing. They were not trying to vindicate Rodney King or to protest injustice. There was nothing righteous about their anger. This was about greed, opportunism and cynicism. But more than that it was about alienation.

These were people who have been consistently denied opportunity in this society, or who are so detached from the mainstream that they can't see the opportunities that are open to them. They were people who feel so disconnected, so lacking a stake in the larger society that their way of interacting with it is to rip it off and burn it down. You despise us, so we'll despise you back. You beat Rodney King and others of our kind, so we'll beat you. These are typical actions of the despised, to turn on others as well as on themselves.

But there were also good things that came out of the Rodney King case. The lawlessness we saw on the streets of L.A. was an aberration, not the norm. Most black people grappled with their anger over the verdict without taking to the streets. They vented their disgust at home, over the telephone, at work, in church, in small groups of friends, and they called for justice. And there were many whites, Latinos and Asians who shared their anger.

Like all great news stories, this one had its share of both malfeasance and redemption. The not-normally-articulate Rodney King summed up the situation when he stuttered his hope that it really is possible for everyone to get along if we only try to work things out.

The verdict and the rioting in Los Angeles were a wake-up call to America to face up to its racial problems. We have heard such calls before, in Watts, Bensonhurst, Howard Beach, but too often we have gone back to sleep.

What happened in Los Angeles was a failure to acknowledge humanity. The police officers who beat Rodney King like a dog denied him his humanity. The jury that acquitted them denied it again. The rioters denied the humanity of those they beat, killed and robbed. And for decades this country has denied the humanity of millions of people who want to work, to enjoy some of life's privileges, and to be counted as part of the whole. It is a vicious cycle that needs to be broken.

For a moment last week, Greg Williams broke the cycle. When asked why he risked grievous harm to save an Asian man he didn't even know, Williams said: "I did it for me . . . Because if I'm not there to help someone else, when the mob comes for me, will there be someone there to save me?"

No Price Tag on Humiliation
SEPTEMBER 28, 1992

If I were a landlord with an apartment to let, I'd rent it to Don Singleton in a minute.

Well-dressed, intelligent, gentle in demeanor and a person who carries with him a quiet elegance, Singleton also happens to have a good job with a bank and a stable rent history. But when he went to look at an apartment in Bay Ridge, Brooklyn, in August 1991, here's what he says happened:

Helen Farhoud, who manages the building at 1618 Owl's Head Court for the co-owners, her husband, Thabit Farhoud, and his uncle, Ahmad Ahad, took one look at Singleton and told him the apartment was rented. Singleton had spoken to her on the phone only minutes before and was assured the apartment was available. But confronted with this slender, quiet, dark-skinned black man, Helen Farhoud suddenly changed her story. In those few minutes, Helen Faroud said, a man from Florida had come to see the apartment, left a deposit, and she had promised him the lease.

"I sat down on the sofa," Don says, remembering how he felt afterward. "I guess you know what's going on, but you don't want to believe it. I kept going through my mind, trying to give her the benefit of the doubt. But the only reason that made sense was that she didn't want to rent to a black person. I felt humiliated, angry, rejected. I felt like somebody of low character, who shouldn't be there in that neighborhood, that I was born to live in the neighborhood where I already lived, that was my lot in life."

After the encounter with Farhoud, Singleton, who had admired the neighborhood when he first arrived there, suddenly felt unsafe and threatened in Bay Ridge. Rather than walk back to the subway, he got a friend to drive him.

The next week Singleton filed a complaint with the Open Housing Center, which sent black and white testers to try to rent Farhoud's apartment. Farhoud told the black tester the same story she told Singleton. She offered the apartment to the white tester, a man of similar age and credentials as Singleton.

Singleton filed a lawsuit against the Farhouds in federal court, charging racial discrimination. A month after the lawsuit was filed, Helen Farhoud filed a complaint with the police, claiming that during their meeting Singleton had forced her into the apartment, twisted her arm, and pressed her against the wall with his body. In a deposition she gave later, she claimed his genitals were exposed. A year later, just before Singleton's lawsuit was to come to trial, Helen Farhoud accused Singleton of attempting to rape her.

"It got progressively worse," Singleton said. "I heard about the assault charge and everybody told me she wouldn't get away with it. But when I heard about the rape charge, I was catatonic for three days."

A young man goes to rent an apartment, is turned away because he's black, and then to beat a discrimination rap, the manager claims he tried to rape her. Does this sound familiar? Like Charles Stuart in Boston, who murdered his pregnant wife, claiming a black guy did it? Or a couple of white hookers in the South trying to avoid arrest for prostitution by accusing nine black men of raping them? The only thing that kept Don Singleton from becoming a modern day Scottsboro Boy is the fact that there are laws on the books forbidding discrimination, and there are people in our legal system who recognize that Don Singletons get screwed simply because they're black.

Last week Singleton's lawsuit was settled when the Farhouds agreed to pay him and his lawyers $50,000 and to make future vacant apartments open to nonwhites. After two days of testimony, the Farhouds realized how outrageous their bigoted behavior and blatant lies would look to a jury, and caved in.

The lesson of this story is that racial discrimination in housing is a virulent practice in 1992, and that its long history is the reason New York City is one of the most segregated cities in the country. Recent census data show that New York City neighborhoods are as racially segregated now as they were a decade ago. Moreover, the housing patterns have very little to do with class or income and everything to do with race. Blacks earning $100,000 a year are as segregated from whites on their income level as blacks living in poverty are segregated from poor whites. And the reason for this is not so much that blacks choose to live among their own, as that whites intentionally keep blacks out of white neighborhoods.

There's always an excuse for why the black guy wasn't sold the house or why the black family wasn't rented the apartment. But trumping up a rape charge takes depravity to new level.

The only way to stop discrimination is to punish the people who engage in it. The $50,000 Singleton won may sound like a lot of money, but not after it's split with the lawyers. And considering what the Farhouds put Singleton through, it's only a trifle. It wasn't just the humiliation of being denied an apartment he was entitled to, or blatantly being lied to, or even being falsely charged with a serious crime. The primary abuse the Farhouds heaped on Don Singleton was the body blow to his self-esteem, the refusal of his entitlement to get what he had earned and was willing to pay for, and the denial of his right to ever again feel secure in this world. If black people so often seem to be angry and discontent, to be carrying an imaginary chip on their shoulders, this is why.

Landlords, real-estate agents and other property owners who discriminate shouldn't pay just $50,000. They should pay $500,000 or a million dollars. We should make them hurt real bad, the way Don Singleton was hurt.

Wisdom from a "Madwoman"

MARCH 2, 1994

Lani Guinier walked into the huge classroom at Columbia University's Law School yesterday and received a warm round of applause. Only a few months ago, she was being vilified as the Morticia of the legal profession. She was Clinton's Quota Queen, her critics said, and she was described by one newspaper as a madwoman.

Funny, but yesterday she didn't look like a witch. She wore a conservative dark green suit, and that famous wild cloud of hair—so often the butt of jokes—was pulled back into a prim bunch of curls.

After Bill Clinton nominated her to head the Civil Rights Division of the Justice Department, Guinier was run out of town by people who thought she had peculiar ideas. She wrote about concepts like cumulative voting, a skewed version of the one-person-one-vote idea, which she said could help protect the interests of minorities.

Calling these ideas downright un-American, the conservatives sent her packing.

You would expect Guinier to be popular in a liberal enclave like Columbia on the Upper West Side of Manhattan. But as she gave a speech defending her ideas, her words echoed loudest in a most unlikely spot—the city's most conservative borough, Staten Island.

This week, the state's Staten Island Charter Commission submitted a bill to the Legislature to allow the island to secede from New York City. It calls for the election of Staten Island's own mayor, controller and 15-member City Council.

It would also create a Staten Island Board of Education, to be elected by . . . could it be? . . . cumulative voting.

"We reviewed a number of possibilities and came up with cumulative voting," says Joseph Viteritti, who headed the commission staff that researched how secession might work.

"I personally think it's the most creative and most imaginative thing we did in the whole process."

Staten Island, you may remember, was the borough that

took the mayoralty from David Dinkins and gave it to Rudolph Giuliani. Of all the boroughs, it is the whitest (80 percent). So why is Staten Island adopting the voting plan of a whacko Quota Queen?

Viteritti said the 13 commissioners were concerned about giving the island's minorities (8 percent black, 8 percent Latino, and 4 percent Asian-and-others) at least some input in the running of an independent Staten Island.

The voting would work like this: In electing the nine-member Board of Education, Staten Island voters would each get nine votes that they could use as they pleased. They could give one vote to each of nine candidates, nine votes to a single candidate, or split their nine votes among several candidates.

In other parts of the country, it has been demonstrated that cumulative voting helps minorities pool their votes and thus get some of their own candidates elected. It prevents them from simply being swallowed up by the majority.

It helped in Alamogordo, N.M., where Chicanos made up 40 percent of the population, but where a Chicano had never been elected to the City Council. When cumulative voting was adopted for City Council elections in 1987, the Chicanos elected their first councilperson.

It also helped the Native Americans in Sisseton, S.D., who were only a third of the population, elect their first school board member.

"It's unfortunate that Lani Guinier was so misunderstood," Viteritti said. "I'm really a supporter of hers. If you read her stuff, it is first-rate and it is not provocative. Her work is good and innovative, and it gets results." He said he had researched the concept of cumulative voting thoroughly and had come to support it even before Guinier was thrust into the public spotlight.

"When we presented the [cumulative-voting] idea to the commissioners, they were very receptive."

Lani Guinier stood before the students and faculty at Columbia and described how her ideas were distorted by her critics and the media. "I was defined entirely by my opponents and those in the media who took control of my image," she said. "Even my mother could not recognize me.

"I came to represent America's worst fears about race," she

continued. Yet, she said, she was trying to do only one thing when she proposed alternate ways of voting. And that was to make sure that minorities could have at least some input in their own governance.

For suggesting something so radical, Guinier was sent back to the University of Pennsylvania Law School, where she continues to teach.

How ironic that Staten Island, the most conservative of places, has now found wisdom in the ideas of a madwoman.

He Wasn't Hindered by Fears

APRIL 5, 1993

He came to the door slowly, his gait wobbly due to a bad leg.

He was a small, round man, his thinned-out hair gone gray, a pair of eyeglasses framing his round, kindly face. He opened the door and let me into his house, a small, yellow frame house with a red awning. The house sat on a quiet street in a modest neighborhood on the outskirts of Birmingham, Ala. William C. Patton, 82, didn't look like a revolutionary, but in such simple places as these can heroes be found.

In 1956, Patton was head of the Alabama NAACP when state officials won a court order enjoining the group from operating in the state. Alabama claimed the organization wasn't properly registered as a legal corporation, but in fact Alabama officials were upset because the NAACP was pushing to desegregate Alabama schools after the Supreme Court in 1954 declared segregated schools unconstitutional.

"I was ordered to turn over our state membership list, but I refused," says Patton, who was convinced that doing so would put the members in danger. For this act of defiance he was ordered to pay a $100,000 fine.

To get around the court order, the NAACP moved its office to Memphis, and Patton worked out of there for eight years until the U.S. Supreme Court ruled that Alabama was wrong in barring the NAACP. At the height of the civil-rights movement, he was the NAACP's national director for political action, and for years he traveled 30,000 miles a year, living out of a suit-case, registering blacks to vote and making sure they got to the polls on election day. He retired from the NAACP in 1978.

I went to Patton's home to talk with him about the changes that have taken place in Birmingham since I was growing up there in the 1950s and 1960s. This week marks the 25th anniversary of Martin Luther King Jr.'s death, so a lot of people are waxing philosophical about the changes King helped bring about. Journalists have been beating a path to Patton's door to talk about King, the movement and the old days.

It's hard for me to convince people that as recently as the 1960s, living in Birmingham was like living under apartheid. Today blacks there live with a much greater degree of dignity, due largely to the efforts of people like W.C. Patton.

"This didn't come easy," Patton told me. "Back then I lived in this same house. I got a lot of phone calls that this house would be bombed. I came out of a lot of meetings and was told I'd be arrested in the morning. At that time it was dangerous to register to vote.

"It didn't come easy at all. But I thank God that I had a part in it, that I'm not yet pushing up the roses, and that I wasn't hindered by my fears."

I sat and listened to Patton and marveled at the years of tedious work and sacrifice that were given by people like him to make this country a place that, while still not free from racial prejudice, is dramatically different from the Birmingham I grew up in.

I fled from Birmingham after high school, trying to escape from the provinciality and the racial meanness of the place. But I admire the people who stayed. People like W.C. Patton, and my parents—a schoolteacher and a principal, who raised their own children there, educated other children, taught us that the world had possibilities beyond those we could immediately see, weathered the political and social battles, and nudged Birmingham into the modern world.

You don't read much about people like these, and their lives aren't featured in the movies or on TV docudramas. But they are the ones who quietly brought about a revolution in this country.

In Birmingham's City Hall, where a black mayor now presides, W.C. Patton's picture hangs on the wall in the gallery of Birmingham's most distinguished citizens. He has received 137 awards for his work over the years, "but they don't mean anything to me," he said.

What excites him is the work he's doing now, at 82, with Birmingham's black children. Every year he takes a group of high school students to visit prisons around the state, where they talk to the inmates and are able to get a sense of the kind of lives they don't want to lead. And this year he helped organize a variety show at the municipal auditorium, where 1,200 high school kids will compete in a talent show for prizes.

"What means something to me is to encourage these young people to be somebody," he said.

Exiles Stand to Vote, Count the Fallen

APRIL 27, 1994

In the end it was such a simple thing. You took a slip of paper, marked an X by the names of your choice, and surrendered your ballot. It took, perhaps, a minute, but it set the woman's hands to shaking.

"When I went in there and they gave me the envelope, I started shaking so much I couldn't hold the crayon," she said. "I couldn't believe this was me."

She was a teacher who fled South Africa for New York City in 1976, after the world's most soulless government began shooting down schoolchildren in the street. In South Africa she had criticized the government for not educating black children, and for this she went to jail several times. Once she spent three weeks in solitary confinement.

"This is for the children who died in 1976," Moli Ntuli said yesterday, becoming one of many South Africans who voted here in New York City and who could compute body by body and day by day the cost of exercising this privilege.

Mamazane Xulu is a social worker who also fled South Africa in 1976. She could remember 20 people she once knew who died in prison or were otherwise murdered by the South African police. Of course, there were also her 18 years in exile. When she filled out her ballot, her hands shook too.

Mxolisi Mgxashe, a man of 50 who is now a teacher and journalist, spent two years in prison as a young man for working with an outlawed political party. When he got out he moved to the United States, where he has spent 27 years in exile.

"Voting was exciting," Mgxashe said, "but at the same time I thought it was not such a big deal after all. I thought, why did so many people have to die for it? Why did Mandela have to spend so many years in prison . . . for this?"

Watching the South Africans vote reminded me of a famous Norman Rockwell painting. It shows a small black girl, no more than 6 or 7, being escorted to school by four white federal marshals. They are tall and she is very small, and she walks to school past a wall scrawled with racial epithets.

There is a lack of symmetry in this painting, between the child's desire merely to attend school, and a state's desire to keep her out, just as there was a lack of symmetry between these South Africans' wish to vote and the price they paid to do so.

No one has completely computed the toll that brought them to the polling places this week. But here are some numbers. In the Sharpville Massacre in 1960, South African police gunned down 69 people who dared to protest against apartheid. The 1976 riot in Soweto, which was started by schoolchildren who opposed being forced to study the Afrikaans language, resulted in 575 people being killed by South African security forces over a period of eight months. During the state of emergency imposed by the government between 1985 and 1990, 20,000 South Africans were detained in prison, often without formal charges being filed against them.

Throughout the 1960s and 1970s, more than 100,000 South African blacks were arrested each year under the infamous Pass Laws. Since the first Pass Laws were initiated by the British in 1916, until they were abolished in 1986, more than 17 million South Africans were prosecuted under them. Since 1984, 20,000 South Africans have been killed as a result of political violence, including 4,400 who died last year.

To Moli Ntuli, Mamazane Xulu and Mxolisi Mgxashe, the cost of voting was as incomprehensible as the need for four white men with guns to escort 6-year-old Ruby Bridges to a Louisiana school in school in 1960. Yet others feared that civilization would crumble if a child went to school or if all the citizens of a country were treated like human beings.

Mgxashe, the journalist who spent two years in prison, knows there are still uncounted casualties of his struggle to vote. Millions of people who are homeless. Millions of people who are unemployed. Millions of youths who have dropped out of school to join the movement. I don't have any illusions that this act will, like a magic wand, solve all the problems created by apartheid.

This was why the making of some Xs on a piece of paper, such a simple thing, was so gut-wrenching for Moli Ntuli, the schoolteacher.

This was for the children who died in 1976.

A Need for Answers

DECEMBER 20, 1993

A defining moment at the Nation of Islam rally this weekend came when Minister Jamil Muhammad took up the collection.

Muhammad is charismatic and he worked the room like an auctioneer. "Who will give $500 to support the ministry of the Rev. Louis Farrakhan?" he asked the 20,000 or so people who were gathered in the hall.

Sister Marie Brooks stepped forward first with $500, followed by Jumal Ali, several anonymous donors, a clothing store in the Bronx called Underground Outerwear, and Scott Gaylin, who topped them all with $1,000.

When Muhammad called for $100 donors, the names seemed to go on forever: Ron 2X Wills from Philadelphia, Raymond Muhammad, Sister Keisha, Akin Jackson, Janice Smith, Lenora Fulani, the NAACP, the black law students of Newark, Luck's Barber Shop, Henrietta Norris, the City College Sons of Africa Association . . . and many others.

Muhammad told the rest of the crowd that if they wanted to support Farrakhan's ministry, they should stand up, reach in their pockets for some money, and wave the bills over their heads in a show of unity. Soon the hall was a sea of hands waving $20, $10 and $1 bills.

Knowledge Infinite Allah, a 16-year-old from New Rochelle, waved a dollar over his head. It is saying something about a teenager that he has traveled all the way from Westchester County, paid $20 to hear Farrakhan, and is still willing to give more. In this slight young man can be seen an explanation for Farrakhan's appeal.

"Islam's message to me is to have pride in my color, to learn everything I can, because to know all things is to be all-powerful," Knowledge said. "That's why I read."

Knowledge (whose family name is Gibbs) was holding two books: a collection of writings by Elijah Muhammad and a hefty tome called Matrix III, which contained chapters on numerology and essays with titles like "Psycho-Social Aspects of Poverty." This last essay, Knowledge said, was about the way the government brainwashes people.

He told me about some of the ideas from his reading—his belief that the U.S. government lies about many things, and his conviction that the AIDS epidemic was created by humans and intentionally planted in the black and gay communities.

We may dismiss such musings as mere cant, but the impressive thing to me was not the quality of Knowledge's knowledge, but the fact that he is seeking knowledge at all. If you know any teachers, you know how hard it is to get a 16-year-old to read, especially something serious. Yet this young man had a hunger for learning.

Many black people, who see so many of their own being sucked into the abyss, and who hear endlessly bad press about themselves, want to understand what exactly is going on. We need a context in which to interpret our condition, and for some Louis Farrakhan provides that.

He speaks to the desolation of the black spirit. For as we know from a recent *Newsweek* article, even upper-middle-class blacks are angry and discouraged by the inequities they experience every day.

Farrakhan says: The problem is not with you. It stems from your long history of being abused. Racism is at the root of your ills, even your bad behavior. But you must stop being a hostage to it. Understand what racism has done to you, and take charge of your life. Get off the drugs and alcohol. Start your own businesses. Embrace marriage and the family. Kick the criminals out of your neighborhoods. In short, whites created niggers, but you don't have to be one.

Part of Farrakhan's message is ugly, and some consider it extreme. There is plenty of cant here too, as when he railed the other night about an alleged conspiracy to portray Michael Jackson as a child molester (because he's becoming too politically aware, Farrakhan said).

He cited the existence of 70 million drug addicts as proof of the growing decadence of American society. He took his usual hit at homosexuals. And in the past he's been bitterly accusatory of Jews and Israel, though he made no such comments Saturday.

It is easy to dismiss Farrakhan's message because it's so extreme. But his strength is that he confronts America with some bitter truths. For if our government can conduct cruel experiments on black syphilis victims, bug the bedrooms of civil rights leaders, and lie about its misdeeds in Panama and Nicaragua, why is it so farfetched that it could go after a rock singer?

Unlike other black leaders, who offer no program for lifting the fortunes of black America, Farrakhan offers one as conservative as any the Republican Party could devise—family values, religion, entrepreneurship, clean living. The difference is that with Farrakhan white America is the target, whereas with the Republicans it's everybody who's not white.

Columbia University professor Manning Marable says it is unfortunate that Farrakhan's critics focus on his racial message, while ignoring the underlying reasons for the rage and alienation that blacks feel.

Given America's denial that its treatment of blacks is as bad as it is, young men like Knowledge Infinite Allah and the others who were waving their money the other night, will continue to seek the truth from Farrakhan, and from wherever else they think they might find it.

Chapter 7

Lawmakers, heartbreakers

All Trained, Nowhere to Go

JUNE 1, 1994

At this very moment, there are two groups of people sitting around Washington, D.C., talking about how they're going to reform welfare.

One group says 1) throw people off the welfare rolls after a couple of years and 2) don't give extra money to unmarried mothers who bear more children.

The other group says yes, go ahead and chuck people off welfare after two years—but train them so they can get jobs and take care of themselves.

We smile when we hear this—it sounds so much like the right thing to do.

But the idea of training people for jobs sounds less promising when you hear the story of Christina Hamler, 23, who has never collected a penny in welfare and has borne no children at all. All she wants is a job and a shot at a career.

Christina went to high school in the suburbs and stayed in school until her senior year. Then family and money problems (plus, she says, a lousy guidance counselor) got the best of her. She dropped out, but went back the very next year, 1989, and got her high school equivalency diploma.

In high school, Christina always worked. She babysat for neighbors and handed out free lunches in a summer-job program for teenagers. She worked as a stage manager for her school district, helping to organize plays, beauty pageants and concerts at her high school. She worked nights and weekends, and for this she was paid $10 an hour.

After she got her diploma, she went looking for a career, but like most high school graduates, found only a job. It was with a real estate firm, screening people who wanted to buy time-shares in condominiums. Occasionally, she even got to take the customers on a tour of the full-scale condo model that was in her office building. With overtime, Christina took home as much as $400 a week.

That job vanished along with New York's real-estate boom, after nobody wanted to buy time-shares anymore. Christina moved to Queens with her boyfriend, and they fixed up a basement apartment. They removed tons of garbage, put up their own walls and laid their own carpets.

One day, her boyfriend saw a commercial for a job-training course in TV production. He told Christina about it, and she liked the idea of a career doing camera work or managing TV shows, just as she had managed the shows at her high school.

She enrolled at the Center for the Media Arts in Manhattan, and took out a $7,600 loan to pay for the six-month course.

"The course wasn't good at all," Christina said. "We had to do videotape editing and some of the editing machines were broken. If I wasn't the first one in the room, I'd have to wait. I worked with a camera about 15 hours in the whole six months. I was trying to do my own story about gun control, and I got it mostly finished, but the tapes we were using were old and used, and had some bad spots in them."

Christina completed the course in January 1991, but got no certificate because she owed the school money: She couldn't keep up her $200-a-month loan payments. For a while, she kept in touch with the school's placement office. Through the school, she got interviews with several TV stations. But they all told her the same thing: She didn't have enough education; she needed some college.

For the next few months, she called the school placement office every day, and they usually said they knew of no jobs. Then for about four months, she called weekly—and was told the same thing. Finally she stopped calling. Last year, the Center for the Media Arts went out of business, after the federal government refused to give any more loans to its students. Too many students didn't pay back the loans, they said— probably because they never got jobs.

After that Christina worked at a couple of department stores, selling jewelry and cosmetics to make ends meet. Then her hours were cut back and she took a job at a baking company in Queens, where her boyfriend worked. She worked in stock and as a cashier for a year, taking home about $268 a week until they, too, cut her hours.

Meanwhile, her boyfriend had bought a computer. Christina studied the manuals and taught herself about such basics as DOS and Windows. She heard that LaGuardia Community College was offering a free three-month course to train women to do computer repairs. Christina signed up.

"I took the ball and ran with it. They gave good information and it appealed to me. There were 30 women in the class, but the number dropped to 12 by the end of the course. I don't know why half of them were there. I would get 95 or 100 on the tests, while some people would get 26."

A lot of the women in her class were on welfare and had children to care for and boyfriends who didn't want them to be there.

"But I wanted to be there," Christina said, "and my boyfriend had no problem with it."

She finished the course in June, 1993, and got a certificate and two awards for her performance. LaGuardia got her an interview with IBM, but the interviewer told her she needed a college degree to get a job. She sent resumes to a lot of other places and made calls to businesses she saw listed in the phone book.

In February, LaGuardia invited her back to take a five-week course in computer networking. She completed the course in March. Then she took a test to become a certified computer network administrator. It took her three tries, but she finally passed the test. Last month, she got her certificate and became the first woman from the LaGuardia program to be certified.

In the last two weeks, Christina has gone to three job interviews, but at each place she was told she needed either more education or more job experience.

Yesterday, she sent me a list of the last 100 jobs she has applied for or inquired about. The list is remarkable for its detail: which newspaper contained the want ad, the job description, the firm's address, who she talked to there, what the interviewer told her, whether she ever heard from them again.

A sampler of how things ended:

Said would call back, didn't.

Need car.

Need two years' experience.

Filled.

Hiring slowly.

No permanent positions.

Given her experience, Christina finds it hard to get excited about the president's promise to train people he wants to get off welfare.

"I've been through three or four training programs and I haven't found anything. I'm not what the companies are looking for. They don't get excited that you went through a training program. They want to know if you have an education or some actual experience. They don't want any quick-education courses. They say, 'You've done a lot, but in the final analysis you haven't really done much at all.'"

If she had to relive the last few years, Christina says, she would go to college. If you consider the time she's put into training courses, it would amount to two years of college anyway, she says.

And now I don't feel I can go to college, because I borrowed all that money and I'm in debt, and I need to work because my boyfriend has been paying all the bills.

In Washington, the president and some legislators talk about training people to get them off welfare. But if this country can't provide a job for someone as highly motivated as Christina, how can it expect to find jobs for all the rest?

Just Keep It Simple, Pat

JULY 25, 1994

Years ago a friend of mine went to an academic conference where Sen. Daniel Patrick Moynihan was one of the speakers.

She mostly went to mingle, and meet men, but the Moynihan speech was part of the package. The speech was some esoteric thing about social reform and why some people are poor. Anyway, midway through the speech, Moynihan veered off into an analogy from Alice in Wonderland.

"What's he talking about?" my friend asked, turning in amazement to the man next to her, a noted academic.

"Nobody knows," he said.

"Then why are all these people just sitting here instead of walking out?" my friend asked.

That is a good question, and one that should be applied to Moynihan's most recent verbal offense—which he caused by referring to the impact of the nation's epidemic of out-of-wedlock births as a kind of speciation.

The senator seemed to suggest that this trend may be spawning a whole new array of social problems. Anyway, it made people mad, since he appeared to be libeling blacks and stirring up notions of genetic inferiority and subhuman racial traits.

What was Moynihan talking about? The problem is Moynihan's own version of Don't Ask, Don't Tell: Not only does anybody not understand what he means when he talks this way, but nobody asks, and the senator doesn't bother to tell.

Moynihan's pronouncements have been offending people for ages, certainly since 1965, when he sounded an alarm about the disintegrating black family, and five years later when he created a firestorm of criticism with his benign neglect argument on the issue of race.

Most people who hate him for these remarks have never bothered to read what he wrote or to try to understand what he was saying about the black family, or racial rhetoric or teenage pregnancy.

We just know we don't like the sound of it, even though thoughtful folks, including Martin Luther King, Jr., Jesse Jackson and the folks at the NAACP and the Urban League, have echoed some of the same sentiments.

Voting in the U.S. Senate, Daniel Moynihan has more often than not acted with a commendable social conscience. But when he speaks, he drives right-thinking people into a frenzy.

Part of Moynihan's problem is his arrogance and his air of paternalism. He makes pronouncements about certain groups, but his remarks are aimed at the ears of an elite of academics and statesmen. Nor does he sully his hands by mingling with the people he's talking about to explain what he really means.

"He's a very misunderstood person," says Phillip Thompson, a professor of political science at Barnard College and professor of public administration at Columbia's business school.

"If you look at his record and read what he's written about

carefully, it's not bad, even though you may not agree with everything. He is at least very frank about some controversial issues."

The problem is, when do you get to talk to him about it? He doesn't interact—not just with blacks, but with any community folks or local elected officials. You invite him to things and he doesn't show up. I think the problem isn't so much the content of what he says as much as it is a matter of his personal style.

Add to this the fact that almost nobody bothers to ask Moynihan what he really means. The senator, along with William Buckley, are the two social commentators almost nobody understands. They quote from obscure tomes none of us has read. Their ramblings are so full of sophomoric pomposity that they insist on talking about today's problems through parables harking back to the 19th century.

Moynihan makes considerably more sense than Buckley, who has been rambling unchecked for years, but we are so intimidated by his intellectual veneer that we're afraid to ask, like my friend, "What is he talking about?"

So Moynihan makes his speeches, drapes his cloak about him, and vanishes into the night, leaving us confused. He doesn't bother to hang around to explain to us what he meant.

Aloof and clinical, in love with his numbers and his books, he also lacks suggested solutions, and seems to lack the compassion that acknowledges that these are real people he's talking about, and not ciphers.

We should demand that the senator speak to us in a language we understand. After all, we are smarter than he thinks, if only because, not observing the world from his lofty height, we understand it better.

Yo, Pat, what's up with this? That way, all of us would learn a lot.

Three-Strikes Law Strikes Out
MARCH 7, 1994

Larry Fisher is a jerk and a screw-up.
In and out of jail since he was a teenager, he was convicted

of his first adult felony in 1986, after he knocked his grand-father down and took $390 from the old man. He spent three months in jail for the crime.

In 1988, Fisher robbed a pizza parlor of $100 by sticking his finger under his jacket and pretending he had a gun. He did 17 months in prison for that.

Last January, Fisher struck again, holding up a convenience store with the old finger-under-the-jacket routine. His take was $151.

Fisher, 35, is now considered a three-time loser in his state of Washington, and, if convicted of this last robbery, he faces a mandatory sentence of life in prison without the possibility of parole.

Under the former Washington law, Fisher might have gotten 22 months in prison. But last fall the people of Washington passed a three strikes law, which requires that people con-victed of three felonies go to jail for life.

The Washington law is truly stupid, since it makes no distinction between violent career criminals and a punk like Fisher. But it is part of a growing clamor for three-strikes laws all over the country.

Gov. Mario Cuomo has called for a three-strike law in New York, and President Bill Clinton plans to introduce one in Con-gress for those convicted of federal crimes. Currently, there are more than a dozen three-strike bills pending in Congress.

The Cuomo and Clinton bills make more sense than the Washington law, since they would apply only to violent felons—people who commit crimes such as murder, rape, armed rob-bery and kidnapping. But they are still a bad and hypocritical idea.

The public is fed up with crime in general and with the misdeeds of repeat offenders in particular. One of the horrors of the Polly Klaas murder case in California, where a 12-year-old girl was abducted from her home and later found mur-dered, was that her accused murderer, Richard Allen Davis, had two prior convictions for kidnapping, and had been re-leased from prison early in both cases.

If he hadn't been on the streets, people said, Polly Klaas would be alive today. The politicians, smelling a hot issue, have gone overboard. Commit three violent felonies, they say, and you go to prison forever.

However, three-strike laws are redundant and unnecessary. They are being called for because prison terms in this country have never meant what they claim to mean, and therefore there is no truth in sentencing.

The average person convicted of murder in the United States serves 6.9 years in prison, the average rapist, 4.5 years, the average person convicted of aggravated assault, 1.9 years. Of course their official sentences are much longer, but because of liberal rules regarding parole and good time, almost nobody serves a full sentence.

The reason for this is financial. Nationally, it costs about $20,000 a year to keep someone in prison. The politicians love to holler lock 'em up, and some governors like Mario Cuomo have made a career of building prisons. But pretty soon it becomes too expensive. You send the criminals away, but then you find excuses to let them out. It is a game played with mirrors.

New York State, for example, has some of the toughest sentences for felonies in the nation. But it also has parole. If you get a five- to 15-year sentence, you must serve at least five years. After that, the Parole Board can decide whether you're sufficiently rehabilitated to get out of prison or whether you should stay in longer.

But after you've served two-thirds of your maximum, you get out of prison automatically, provided you haven't messed up while in prison. That's called good time, and it means that a prison sentence is New York State is worth only two-thirds of what it claims to mean.

In the federal system, they have eliminated parole altogether and severely restricted the amount of good time prisoners can earn. The state politicians ought to push for real reforms like the feds, instead of talking about three-strike laws.

Richard Girgenti, New York State's director of criminal justice, says we need a three-strike law because there's no way to guarantee that a three-time violent criminal won't strike again, unless you put him or her in prison for life.

Why did we let them out of prison in the first place? A 15- or

20-year sentence will keep a violent criminal out of action about as well as a life sentence, if you actually make them serve it. By the time they're released, they will probably be too old to be interested in committing any more crimes.

We could then release them into the world, instead of turning our prisons into nursing homes.

The clamor for three-strike laws is all about politics and the failure of nerve. The politicians don't want to spend the money to keep violent criminals in jail for the duration of their sentences.

When they get out and strike again, the politicians express outrage at the recidivists they have let out of prison too soon. Three-strike laws are their way of saving face. It's pretending to be doing something, when you're really doing nothing much.

What Are Joint Chiefs Afraid Of?

JANUARY 27, 1993

Hank Carde's career in the U.S. Navy was brilliant.

During the 20-year tour of duty that took him to San Diego, Japan, Korea and Vietnam, he drove ships ranging from tiny minesweepers to super aircraft carriers. He became one of the Navy's youngest intelligence specialists. During his three tours in Vietnam, he ran spy-nets behind enemy lines and worked with the elite special forces known as the SEALS.

In Vietnam's Forest of Darkness, a 30-by-50-mile stretch of dense mango swamp from which French battalions had never escaped alive, he stuck it out with Naval Special Forces. They rode river rain boats up the canals, carrying supplies and ammunition to U.S. fire bases. Every week, four boats went in, and every week, one of the boats got blown away. Carde's job was to detect mines and ferret out sappers—the enemy engineers who set the traps.

He won two Bronze Stars and rose to the rank of commander. His last job was strategic planning policy director on the staff of Adm. William Crowe, then head of the Joint Chiefs of Staff. In 1988, he was offered the command of his own destroyer, but he retired from the Navy to tend to his companion, who was dying of AIDS.

For 20 years, Carde kept silent about his homosexuality. Now he loudly gives the lie to the argument that's being urged on President Bill Clinton by the top commanders of the armed forces. They say that lifting the ban on homosexuality in the armed forces would undermine military morale and discipline and disrupt military readiness. One soldier who was interviewed last week said that if the president lifted the ban against homosexuals, the military would have to relabel its bathrooms men, women and third sex. He didn't say where the estimated 10 percent of the military who are homosexual now go to relieve themselves.

"When you're in combat, sex is one of the last things on your mind," Carde says. "You're worried about your unit, your mission, staying alive and keeping your buddies alive. You sit in foxholes in monsoon rains. You try to keep alert and warm and keep from being overrun.

"When you're at sea you're working eight to 12 hours a day, doing four-hour watches. You do exercises and fire drills. You live in close quarters with bunks stacked on top of each other. It's very demanding. Conditions, in short, are not exactly conducive to homosexual trysts."

When Carde was an undergraduate at Yale during the 1960s, outraged alumni used the same argument against the university's proposal to admit women. They were convinced the college would fold, he said. Carde joined the Navy ROTC, and after graduating in 1968 he went straight into a military career. Yale started admitting women the next year, and despite the dire predictions, neither its morale nor its reputation suffered.

During his pre-enlistment interview, and for years thereafter during periodic security checks, Carde was asked if he was gay. He lied and said no, rationalizing that he wasn't really lying because he considered himself to be bisexual. "I felt like I was being asked by the SS in Nazi Germany if I were a Jew." When sailors told fag jokes, he bit his tongue, knowing that to respond would mean being drummed out of the service. And this son of a Navy captain loved the Navy. He considered it his great adventure.

In Yokosuka, Japan, Carde was executive officer—second to the commander—of the ship *Francis Hammond*. He drummed out sailors who broke the ship's rules regarding sexual behavior, whether they were gay or straight. Under his command was a very effeminate sailor who, because of the pressure he was under, tried to commit suicide twice by drinking bleach. Carde didn't let on that he was also gay, but he tried to help the sailor, and arranged for him to see a psychologist. The sailor eventually left the Navy.

During most of his 20 years in the Navy, Carde put his personal life on hold. Then he met his lover, who was a floral designer. It was his lover's illness and Carde's subsequent decision to leave the Navy that brought his long silence to an end.

"This is a matter of justice," he says. "As Americans we should not tolerate discrimination against any other American. I served this country for 20 years in every trouble spot on the globe, defending that principle. At this point I'm not going to let a bunch of bigots demean and conduct witchhunts against the one out of 10 sailors and soldiers who are gay."

The Uniform Code of Military Justice's prohibition on sodomy is enforced almost solely against gay servicemen. Since most of the general public admits to having engaged in oral sex, we can assume that most straight soldiers are breaking the same code that's used to drum gays out of uniform.

Gen. Colin Powell and the commanders-in-chief of all four branches of the armed services told President Clinton this week that homosexuals would only drag the military down. Have any of them met former Navy commander Hank Carde?

While Pork's Improved, Pols Haven't

AUGUST 29, 1994

On his pig farm outside Davenport, Iowa, Glenn Keppy could only shake his head and smile at all the pig talk coming out of Washington these last few weeks.

Keppy, who raises 3,000 pigs for market each year, has never heard so much talk about pork and pork barrels as he has heard recently from the lips of our representatives in Congress.

Sen. Alfonse D'Amato, giving us further proof that New York's junior senator is losing his mind, even made up nasty song lyrics about pork, thereby ruining "Old MacDonald Had A Farm" for several generations of former children.

Opponents of the crime bill used the words pork and pork barrel to attack what they said amounted to political spoils and Democratic excess in the crime bill. Newt Gingrich, whose home state of Georgia is known for its succulent hams, led the charge against the pig.

I was shocked to hear respected members of Congress denouncing the fat in a bill that would do such awful things as give basketballs to kids in the projects and drug treatment to addicts. One anti-fat legislator was Rep. Susan Molinari of Staten Island, who has become a darling of the press, despite her inability to get a coherent sentence out of her mouth.

She and other Republicans were heard to say that the only way to really fight crime is with more police and more prisons. The other stuff was all pork, they said, and therefore both nutritionally and socially unsound.

The Republicans are known for being mean-spirited and short-sighted in the extreme. They will now go down in history as having libeled both the pig and the pork barrel.

Ask Glenn Keppy. "We all take it with a grain of salt when politicians use the term 'pork barrel.' It would be nice if they used a more appropriate term. In the last 15 years, pork has gotten 31 percent leaner. So in reality when they talk about pork they're saying that things are leaner, and I don't believe that's what they're intending to say."

Keppy, who has been in the pork producing business more than 30 years, raises meat hogs, which are pigs bred to be low in fat. Since people stopped using lard for cooking after World War II, the pork industry started breeding leaner pigs. The anti-fat crusade of nutritionists and the medical profession further spurred pork farmers to reduce the fat content in pigs.

To accomplish this, Keppy cross-breeds three kinds of hogs to get the right combination of leanness, rapid growth and breeding ability. He also watches the amount of amino acids and proteins his pigs get in their diet to ensure that they will have a high concentration of meat and a low level of body fat. The result is a lean and mean critter that even a Republican could love.

Audrey Cross, a professor of nutrition at Columbia University's School of Public Health, agrees that today's pig is being maligned in Congress.

"Pork has trimmed down," Cross says. "It really has."

In fact, she says, a trimmed pork chop now contains about the same fat content as a comparable portion of chicken.

Here is her comparison of the relative fat content of pork today versus other meats:

3 oz. roast beef (trimmed)—5.5 grams of fat
3 oz. sirloin—7.4 grams of fat
3 oz. pork loin—4.1 grams of fat
3 oz. fresh ham—9.4 grams of fat
3 oz. skinless chicken—5.6 grams of fat
3 oz. skinless white turkey—2.7 grams of fat

This proves the scurrilousness and duplicity of Congress' attack on pork. However, this is not nearly as scandalous as its attack on the pork barrel.

This term, which is most often used by the party out of power to attack legislation proposed by the party in power, is meant to describe funds that are sought by legislators for their own districts, primarily to ensure that they get re-elected.

Pork barrel is supposed to suggest excess, extravagance, payola. In fact, the term goes back to slavery and refers to those occasions when the slaves assembled, literally, at the pork barrel on the plantation so that Ol' Massa could dole out the helping of pork that was reserved for the slaves.

This periodic doling out of pork was supposed to be a kind of reward to the slaves for their good behavior. But Ol' Massa was not inclined to be extravagant. The slaves' take from the pork barrel were the pathetic leavings after Massa had gutted the hog. At most they got some pigs' feet and some entrails (which through their own skill they turned into the delicacy of chitterlings).

Now some members of Congress suggest that money that is intended to keep kids from growing up to be criminals is nothing but a dip from the old pork barrel. Since some of these kids are the descendants of the original pork barrel recipients, in a way they are right. The greatest portion of the money in the crime bill will be spent on arresting people and locking them up, a much smaller portion on measures to help kids grow up to be good citizens.

I suppose it is the pork barrel approach to crime after all that bears more than a passing resemblance to Ol Massa's.

Kevorkian to the Rescue

MAY 2, 1994

Thomas Hyde was having a miserable life.

Twenty-nine years old and afflicted with Lou Gehrig's disease, his physical condition was rapidly going downhill. His muscles barely functioned and he could hardly get around or feed himself. To his dismay, he couldn't pick up his infant daughter and he scared his young son.

He'd lost control of his tongue and his speech was becoming unintelligible. When he ate, he sometimes choked. He couldn't lie on his back for fear of strangling, and he knew that eventually he would choke to death on his own saliva.

Hyde wanted to die quickly and quietly and avoid further misery, and this was certainly the most merciful end for him.

But he couldn't find a way to commit suicide that was acceptable to him, or that wouldn't involve his friends and relatives. He tried to get morphine, but couldn't. He was too weak to hold a gun. To use the techniques recommended by The Hemlock Society, which often require drugs and a plastic bag, he would have needed help. So he turned to Dr. Jack Kevorkian.

Only Kevorkian, whom some call Dr. Death, would assist him. And without doubt Kevorkian showed Hyde more compassion than anyone else did.

Hearing Kevorkian testify in his own trial for helping Thomas Hyde kill himself is a scary thing. however. He said his only motive in providing Hyde with the carbon monoxide machine with which he committed suicide was to end his suffering.

"Any doctor who's a real doctor . . . would care for nothing, nothing, nothing other than the condition of his patient!" he told the court, defiantly.

The man is a zealot—arrogant, self-righteous, and on a crusade. He is the Ralph Nader of the assisted suicide business.

He is also careening out of control. You realize this when you hear him tell about his efforts to evade the police on the day he helped Thomas Hyde kill himself.

Kevorkian didn't want the suicide to take place at Hyde's home, because he didn't want Hyde's friends and relatives to be implicated. So he started the suicide procedure in a van behind his own apartment. At some point he and his assistant transferred Hyde's body from one van to another in an alley three blocks from Kevorkian's home. They were trying to minimize interruption from the police, he said.

Later, Kevorkian drove Hyde's body to Belle Island on the Detroit River, to avoid rougher treatment from the police in his own neighborhood who were used to his escapades. He was stopped and arrested en route. As you listen, this tale begins to sound like something from a Sherlock Holmes story.

It says a lot about Dr. Kevorkian that he considered his 40-year career as a pathologist a failure until he started helping sick people kill themselves. His proposals—he wanted to transfuse blood from recently deceased corpses and to conduct experiments on condemned prisoners while they were being executed—made him a pariah in the medical profession.

Ironically, helping people die breathed life into his own withering career. Dr. Jack Kevorkian has become a cowboy of the medical profession, riding into town to shoot the mortally wounded, though at their own request, of course. He compares himself to the early anesthesiologists, who defied the law and the church by trying to ease people's pain.

He accuses those who would stop him of having a Dark Ages mentality, and claims he knows at least 10 people whose lives he could have saved if he had been allowed to arrange organ donations from some of the people he helped to commit suicide.

One shudders at the thought of Kevorkian being left to his

own devices, assisting people to commit suicide and then harvesting their blood and organs. Like all zealots, who think they alone are right, and that they are right to break the law in the pursuit of their mission, he is a dangerous man. He moves bodies about in alleyways and leads the police on a chase.

Yet Jack Kevorkian exists because he fills a gap. It's a gap that's created by doctors who refuse to provide enough pain medicine to sick people who are suffering, and who won't supply the drugs with which patients—who wish to die and deserve the escape death provides—could peacefully end their lives.

These are the physicians who preach about a doctor's duty to preserve life, but worry more about turning a patient into a drug addict than about easing unbearable pain. So, in rides Dr. Kevorkian with his carbon monoxide machine and his reckless methods.

It is ironic that in the early days of medicine, doctors were often present at the bedside of their dying patients. Since they were able to offer little in the way of medicines or scientific knowledge to cure illness, ease suffering or forestall death, they could at least show up at the end to comfort the dying and console the family.

These days when physicians have so much technology, knowledge and medicine to offer, they are rarely there when death comes. They have no time for deathbed vigils. They can prolong life beyond the body's usefulness, and when it ultimately starts to deteriorate, they are absent, or can offer only platitudes.

And here comes Jack. He is there and they aren't, and that is their shame and to his credit.

Wrong Cure for Welfare
MARCH 16, 1994

If Mayor Rudolph Giuliani gets his way, New York City will soon begin fingerprinting welfare recipients—taking finger images, as the new technology is called.

"It's inevitable," an administrator in the city's Human Resources Administration said yesterday, adding that it's necessary to cleanse the welfare system of double-dippers—people who use multiple identities to collect more than one welfare check.

Governor Mario Cuomo says he won't object to the Giuliani plan, and since welfare procedures are regulated by state law, fingerprinting seems likely to happen.

It is a bad idea, but not because it discriminates against the poor, or violates their privacy, or makes people submit to an indignity in order to receive public benefits.

It's a bad idea because it's based on specious assumptions about the level of welfare fraud, and because fingerprinting every welfare applicant just to find a few cheats is as productive as using an elephant gun to shoot flies.

Giuliani claims fingerprinting will save the city $89 million in fraudulent welfare payments. But, as New York *Newsday* has reported, this claim is based on a misreading of a tiny study that was done upstate.

For a year and a half, New York State experimented with fingerprinting single adults who were applicants for home relief in two counties, Rockland and Onondaga. After fingerprinting came in, the home relief rolls in these counties, which had been 3,344, dropped by 495 cases. The experiment did not uncover a single instance of anybody double-dipping in the two counties.

The state's Department of Social Services found that 330 cases were closed for routine reasons—clients moving or disappearing. Another 145 cases were closed for no apparent reason except that the clients refused to be fingerprinted. The Department claimed this saved the state $46 million.

Giuliani seized on these numbers, saying that fingerprinting had reduced the welfare rolls in those counties by 15 percent because it had scared away welfare cheats.

But in actuality, home-relief rolls were reduced by only 4.3 percent as a direct result of fingerprinting. There is simply no way to tell whether any of those clients who failed to reapply were double-dippers who feared getting caught, or whether they were simply offended or frightened by the idea of being fingerprinted.

No one knows the real extent of welfare fraud, but available evidence suggests it is small. The state's Department of Social Services estimates that, of the $4 billion spent on welfare and home relief in New York State, perhaps 1 to 3 percent is fraudulently obtained.

This is a lot of money, but if you figure how much it will cost to fingerprint all the welfare applicants in the state, return-on-investment will not be very high. (The Department of Social Services says it would cost $18 million just to get started.)

When we hear stories like the one about the 21 people who were arrested this month for cashing welfare checks in both New York and New Jersey, welfare fraud sounds like a widespread problem. That bust identified 425 welfare recipients who had double-dipped over a period of at least three years, although more than half of them had already stopped double-dipping, and only a few dozen were actually arrested and charged.

According to the city's Human Resources Administration, 200 arrests for double-dipping were made in New York City alone over the last year and a half. But all of these frauds were uncovered through regular police work—not fingerprinting.

Given that New York City has a million welfare recipients, proven cases of welfare fraud are relatively rare. Yet politicians continue to conjure images of welfare queens and lash out at imaginary legions of the Poor and Lazy who thrive by scamming the welfare system.

In her book, *Tyranny of Kindness,* Theresa Funiciello, a former welfare mother, compares the incidences of welfare fraud and income-tax fraud. She notes that the Department of Social Services estimates that fewer than 3 percent of welfare recipients in New York State engage in fraud, while the IRS estimates that 20 percent of all income-tax filers commit fraud—primarily by understating their incomes.

The truth is that the push for fingerprinting is not about eliminating fraud, since there's little evidence that there is much fraud. It's about being punitive. It's about assuming that people on welfare are basically dishonest and shiftless and must be rooted out.

It's a kind of bravado that says: Look at us. We're getting tough with the poor.

The Skeletons
SEPTEMBER 7, 1992

Come on, Gerry. Come clean. Now. Before it's too late.

That's the punchline in a TV ad that's being aired by city comptroller Elizabeth Holtzman, who's running in the New York Democratic primary for the U.S. Senate. In the ad, which has been roundly criticized for being too negative, Holtzman urges rival Geraldine Ferraro to respond fully to charges that Ferraro and her husband benefited financially from ties to organized crime, including receiving rent from a former tenant who was a child pornographer.

Holtzman has also criticized Ferraro for not disclosing her and her spouse's business and tax records—information that first came under scrutiny during Ferraro's 1984 run for the vice presidency.

I've written previously that Holtzman is justified in raising these issues, since questions about ethics and character are relevant in a political campaign. But I also wonder: Would Holtzman really want Ferraro to answer these questions?

Suppose Ferraro held a press conference this week and said in the full glare of the camera lights: "It's true. Throughout our careers my husband and I have knowingly solicited business and campaign contributions from members of the Mafia. Hey, those guys have got big bucks, and even crooks are entitled to good representation in Washington. And, yeah, we kept renting to the pornographer for three years after we learned what he was up to. Why should we hurry up and evict a guy when we can collect another $300,000 in rent by going slow? We're not stupid, you know!"

Even if Ferraro bared her soul about every transgression she has committed since childhood, Holtzman probably wouldn't be satisfied. Come cleaner, Gerry, the new ads would read. You still haven't told all.

That's because the charges leveled against Ferraro belong to the category of political albatrosses. These are rumors and scandals, large or small, substantiated or unproven, that dog a politician for decades, lying around in the closet, smelling up the place.

The politician may try to dispose of them by offering explanations or outright apologies. But they can never completely be rid of them because trying to explain them away only reinforces how real their transgressions were. Also, their critics don't really want answers; they want to keep brandishing the ugly skeletons.

A classic example is Teddy Kennedy. For more than 20 years, he's been tarred by the sticky brush of Chappaquiddick. Every time he's even hinted he might run for president, or been cast in the role of making moral judgments (during the Clarence Thomas hearings), or his decorum has come into question (during his nephew's rape trial), Chappaquiddick reared its ugly head. "What's a suspected philanderer and murderer doing trying to lead the country or sitting in judgment on somebody else," the critics say. "After all, he's never come clean about Chappaquiddick."

Suppose Kennedy went on network TV and said: "Yes, I was trying to hit on Mary Jo that night in 1969, and I was trying to convince her to go with me to a motel when I ran my car off the road and into the river. And, yes, I was so worried about how getting caught with her would affect my career that I ran away and left her to drown. But I deeply regret my behavior and I believe I am a different man than I was 20 years ago."

Would this assuage his critics? I don't think so. They would keep demanding that he give a full explanation of his actions on that fateful night.

For that matter, would Jesse Jackson appease the Jewish community once and for all over his Hymietown remark if he agreed to do penance by crawling on his hands and knees over cut class through the streets of Crown Heights? I doubt it. Jackson can explain and apologize forever, but Hymietown will always dog him.

The most persistent criticism of Bill Clinton is that he's slick and untrustworthy, and that he's never been honest about himself, especially about his personal life.

Suppose Clinton were to come clean. Suppose he admitted publicly that he had an affair with Gennifer Flowers and paid her off by putting her on the Arkansas state payroll. And suppose he admitted he smoked marijuana—and inhaled deeply—

on a number of occasions. Would this silence the demands for Clinton to come forward with the truth about himself? Forget it.

The fact is we're willing to tolerate a certain amount of immorality in our politicians. We assume it goes with the territory. We also know that frailty is human. We recognize our own foibles and potential ethical lapses in those we elect to public office, so to reject them for their screw-ups would be like rejecting ourselves.

We tolerate their transgressions as long as we can be self-righteous about them.

So we urge politicians who we know have gone astray to confess, to come clean. We may know exactly what they did wrong, and understand why they did it. But as long as they remain in public office, or continue to pursue it, we hold their feet to the fire.

I suppose this is a good thing because it means there will be some price to pay when public figures do things they shouldn't. The point is, we don't really care if they come clean or not. We just want to remind them that they've been bad.

Stuck on a Hanger

AUGUST 14, 1991

Victor Delmastro came out of the closet yesterday.

"Is there anything you want to reveal, Victor?" I asked him, searchingly.

"I would like to say I'm proud to be a Catholic," Victor told me. "That's certainly something people don't say enough about."

"Anything else?" I said, probing for more shocking details.

"I consider myself a straight Democrat," he said. "At least I'm trying to run as a Democrat, but they won't let me."

Poor Victor.

In a City Council race that has become the most dazzling in the city due to revelations about the health problems and sexual proclivities of its candidates, Delmastro seems as exciting as oat bran.

He is one of three candidates vying for the City Council seat from District 3, which includes the West Village, Chelsea, Clinton and Soho. The district was recently gerrymandered to create a City Council seat that is friendly to the homosexual populace. This may not bode well for Delmastro, a single, heterosexual male.

Last week, he was upstaged by opponent Thomas K. Duane, a longtime gay activist who announced with great fanfare that he is HIV positive. In revealing this news, Duane said it would be very compelling to have an HIV-positive person on the City Council to represent that group, just as having women, Hispanics and Asians on the council was helpful to those constituencies.

Meanwhile, Liz Abzug, the other contender, declared herself a lesbian and has been appealing to feminist and lesbian sympathies. Is there any other city, save San Francisco, where this could happen? Where a regular guy like Victor Delmastro would be totally overshadowed by folks who at one time would have been considered on the fringe?

But this is New York City in 1991, and Delmastro obviously lacks the credentials to be a compelling candidate. Consider this. He was born 32 years ago in St. Clare's Hospital on 51st Street, and attended Catholic schools, graduating from St. Agnes High School. He received bachelor's and master's degrees in biology from Columbia University and Hunter College. He is a science teacher at Martin Luther King, Jr. High School and is a longtime housing activist in lower Manhattan.

Clearly, these credentials will never get Victor on the "Geraldo" show.

How times have changed. For decades, political candidates hid their illnesses for fear of being perceived as weak or having limited futures. Franklin Roosevelt would only be photographed from the waist up, allowing him to hide his crippled legs. And any evidence of his later debilitating illnesses was carefully hidden from the American public. John F. Kennedy lied outright about having Addison's disease, for fear that it would derail his political career. And in his final campaign for the U.S. Senate, Jacob Javits tried to downplay his Lou Gehrig's disease, although he lost the race anyway and soon afterward succumbed to total disability.

Innuendoes about sexual deviation have also haunted many candidates in the past. Questions about Edward Koch's sexuality were so persistent that he flaunted his friendship with Bess Myerson in order to look like a regular guy. Rumors of lesbianism plagued Carol Bellamy and Elizabeth Holtzman in their political campaigns. Only in recent years has homosexuality emerged as an occasional political asset.

This increased tolerance is a good thing overall. But the irony of how this reversal is being played out in District 3 is a head-spinner.

What's happened in this particular race is that sexual orientation has been politicized—and now health issues are being politicized, says Delmastro, who feels a bit victimized by all the publicity given to Duane and Abzug. He says the purpose of redistricting was to increase the representation of racial and ethnic minorities, not to make sexual orientation an issue.

It serves to divide the gay community, since you have one candidate running as gay, the other as a lesbian, and it's divided the women. He accuses Duane and Abzug of being one-issue candidates and says the publicity given to their revelations has obscured the real issues in the district.

Delmastro's platform, he says, calls for more efficient city spending in lieu of tax increases; the creation of a comprehensive plan for developing the West Side waterfront; and a drastic overhaul of the program for converting city-owned buildings into low land moderate-income housing.

Duane is viewed as the current frontrunner in the District 3 race, Abzug having been roundly criticized as a lesbian-come-lately who embraced the lesbian cause only to further her political ambitions. But Delmastro hopes the sexual issues they have raised will actually help him in the election, by splitting the homosexual and the women's vote.

I mean, what else can a poor, straight, Catholic male hope for?

Chapter 8

New York stories: The garden is still green

Ode to Joy in the Age of Angst

AUGUST 26, 1994

The first time David saw Eileen walk into a room, he thought she was beautiful.

"I'm not going to lie about that, he told me the other day. When I first saw her, I said 'I've got to get to know her.'"

He was working at a Bronx church that ran a food program for people who are HIV-positive. On the day Eileen walked in, he was setting up tables for lunch.

The way Eileen remembers it, she was a mess.

"I was rundown, sick, depressed. I weighed 20 pounds less than I do now," she said. "From not eating, I had no strength. I was living with someone who didn't care, and I wasn't even looking at guys then."

David, who always seemed so busy when Eileen saw him at the church, didn't look sick at all.

He had moved to New York from California in 1981, after a visit to an Army buddy in Howard Beach made him want to stay. He got a job doing home-improvement work with a contractor in Queens, then he met a girl and got married. "I thought she was the best thing there was, but our whole lives revolved around drugs," David said.

His wife's name was Maryann, and he got her name tattooed on his neck, bordered by a star on each side. They shot heroin together, and over time, David started pulling off burglaries to support their habits. For years, he did at least one job a week until he got busted and went upstate for two years. He was diagnosed as HIV-positive after he got out in 1983. (Back then, they still called it the HTLV2 virus.)

Prison had at least one good result for David: he stopped doing drugs. When he got out, he went to the Momentum Project, which gives free food, clothing and other help to the HIV-positive. That's where he met Eileen in 1992.

She was living in a hellhole in the Bronx with a boyfriend she had taken up with several years earlier. The guy was a freak. He moved 22 pet pigeons into the living room of their apartment, and that drove Eileen into the bedroom—where she became a permanent resident.

"I didn't want to come out," Eileen said. "And he was overbearing. He would say 'Why do you want to get your teeth fixed? Who are you going to smile at?' I was out of touch with my friends, my family, everybody."

Eileen, who had done heroin a decade before and had two former boyfriends who died of AIDS, was diagnosed as HIV-positive in 1986. Then she came down with TB and pneumonia. She had thought about leaving her boyfriend, but figured, "I'll stick with him, since I'll be dead in a year."

At the church, she and David started to talk. She was shy and withdrawn, and he tried to draw her out. He invited her to join his discussion group for substance abusers and he took her to various city agencies to apply for benefits. He got her a doctor through his own physician. She told him about her home life. "I couldn't believe anyone could actually live like that," David said.

Last Christmas, David went to California to visit his family. Before he left, he had decided to return to New York, pack his belongings, and move back West. But in California he kept thinking about Eileen.

"I spent Christmas alone," Eileen said.

When he got back to New York, he tried to call her, but she had no telephone. Then they saw each other again at the church. This time, they started seeing each other more often.

In April, David got a studio apartment in Harlem and Eileen moved in with him. He had asked her to marry him on St. Patrick's Day.

"I want to spend the rest of my life with her," he said. "I can't believe there could be anybody else in this world who's more compatible with me. She even loves sports as much as I do."

"I love him very much," Eileen says. "He's clean. He's not into drugs whatsoever. He's sensitive. He thinks about me. He brings me flowers and tells me I look pretty. That's something I hadn't heard in years. He even likes to cook."

As they sat in their cozy apartment this week, they didn't look or behave like people over whom the specter of AIDS hangs so heavily. Eileen, who has long, straight, blond hair, looks plump and healthy. She had a touch of pneumonia last week, but took drugs to keep from going to the hospital.

David, who has long, dark hair and wears an earring in his left ear, had AIDS-related pneumonia back in 1989, but since then has kept himself healthy with antibiotics, vitamins and lots of vegetables.

"The disease is living with me and not the other way around," he says.

Tomorrow, David Harvey, 36, and Eileen Voigt, 39, will be getting married at St. Paul the Apostle Church on 9th Avenue and 59th Street. The people from the Momentum Project are putting together a reception for them, and they got a Bay Ridge, Brooklyn, department store to donate a $1,500 wedding dress for Eileen. She and David have bought plain gold rings for the occasion, and she reached into her closet to pull out the pink organdy dress her niece will wear as flower girl.

"There are days I feel like I don't have the disease," Eileen says, "because I'm so happy. Eight years ago I thought I was going to be dead, and here I am, getting married. If other AIDS patients can read that, maybe they'll come out of their holes like I did."

David wanted to buy her a diamond engagement ring, which would have been a stretch on his $532-a-month Social Security check. But Eileen would hear nothing of it.

"It's not within our means," she said softly.

"I never heard a woman turn down a diamond," David said. "That's one more thing I love about her."

Dream Maker, Heart Breaker

JANUARY 30, 1991

"Where is Harry Lipsig?"

These words issued from the lips of Bebe Herman as she made her way into Brooklyn Civil Court yesterday. Herman was not in a good mood, and it didn't help that she and her daughter-in-law, Irene, had to schlep up the stairs to a crowded second-floor courtroom—with a baby stroller and Herman's almost 2-year-old grandson, Joey, in tow.

For the thousandth time in the last year or so, the question burned in Bebe Herman's brain. "Where is Harry Lipsig?" she asked, and the words had the taste of ashes.

Herman's search for Harry Lipsig began in June, 1989, when her son, Jeffrey, then a 25-year-old New York City police officer, was shot and killed by a man named Albert Smith while investigating a domestic dispute. Smith had recently been set free without bail after being arrested for allegedly kidnapping his girlfriend.

At his arrest, Smith was overheard threatening to kill the next cop he saw, but the assistant district attorney who handled the kidnapping case didn't tell the judge this, possibly because she didn't even know it herself. So the judge let Smith go and he proceeded to murder Jeffrey Herman. Smith later shot himself rather than surrender to the police.

Bebe Herman, bereft of a son, and Irene, suddenly a widow with a 3-month-old baby, were overcome with grief. But anger set in as well when they learned about the negligence that had allowed Jeffrey's killer to walk the streets. So Bebe went looking for Harry Lipsig.

"It seems that every unique case is handled by Harry Lipsig and company," she explained. "He's the man who can make a case."

It was true: Harry Lipsig was not just a lawyer, but a Dream Maker. Already in his 80s and a practicing attorney for more than 60 years, Lipsig was known as the king of personal-injury lawyers. Using chutzpah, meticulous preparation and showbiz glitz, he had a long history of winning the most unlikely cases, raking in millions of dollars in damages for his disabled or bereaved clients, and sometimes literally remaking the law.

There was the $740,000 judgment he won for the family of a heart-attack victim when he convinced a jury the man was frightened to death by a car that rolled onto his lawn. There was the Acapulco hotel that was forced to pay damages to a guest who was attacked by a shark. Lipsig argued that the hotel had dumped garbage into the ocean that had attracted the shark. And there was the $1.25-million judgment the city paid after a psychologist was run over by a squad car driven by a drunken cop. Lipsig convinced the jury that the deceased, who was 71, still had years of earning left. And there were many similar cases.

Bebe Herman found Harry Lipsig in his Manhattan law office, and he agreed to take the case. In fact, Herman said Lipsig was the one who convinced her and her daughter-in-law that they had a case against Brooklyn District Attorney Elizabeth Holtzman, on the grounds that she had failed to properly supervise the staff attorney who handled Albert Smith's case.

"Harry said, 'For you I'm going to do this,'" Herman says. "He said, 'I'm going to make people stand up and take notice. We're going to change the system.' He said this while holding my little grandson on his knee."

Herman says the law firm set up press conferences with the family for local TV stations and milked the case for all the publicity it was worth. "They'd bring my daughter [in-law] in from her home on Long Island and have her waiting for hours for the camera crew . . . They got her all pumped up."

The firm started an investigation of the case and actually filed a lawsuit against the city. But as the months went by, Lipsig ended his longtime partnership with Bonnie Zelman. He formed a new firm and took Mark Manus as a partner. Manus soon wound up with the Herman case. It got so that when the Hermans called the office, they couldn't even get Harry Lipsig on the phone. Herman heard that Harry was ill.

The final blow came last spring when Manus informed them that he felt there was no merit to their case and advised them to drop it.

"Mr. Manus was so rude. He said 'this was not a case, but I'll go through the motions for you' . . . I said, 'Where's Harry. I want Harry' . . . And now Mr. Lipsig has disappeared off the face of the earth."

Mark Manus told me yesterday that his firm did work on the Herman case, and filed a still-pending lawsuit against the city. But over time, he said, the relationship with the Hermans broke down. He says they dismissed him from the case last November, and are completely free to get a new lawyer, if they choose. In fact, he prefers it that way. Yesterday, the parties were due to meet in Civil Court, where Manus had asked to be officially relieved of his duties in the case. The Hermans showed up for the hearing, but Manus did not.

As for Harry Lipsig, now 88, Manus said he has been ailing and recently underwent surgery to have a pacemaker implanted. However, he is in touch with the office by phone every day, Manus said.

I asked Bebe Herman why she and her daughter-in-law don't just hire another lawyer. "We never even thought about getting another lawyer," she said. "My daughter-in-law wants to hear from Harry Lipsig that there is no case, because he's the man who can make a case."

In retrospect, Herman believes the firm used her family to get publicity, because her son's case was so well known, and that they are now being discarded just like a stack of old legal pads. Still, the dream she says was first stirred up by Harry Lipsig fills Bebe Herman's mind, and the hope-filled question lingers on her lips.

As for Harry Lipsig and his law firm, she says: "They led us up a path, and at that particular time in our lives we didn't need any more disappointment or sorrow . . . And now where is Harry Lipsig, besides not being available?"

Freedom Beyond the Hill

AUGUST 18, 1993

Slim, who is tall, rangy and wore a pair of dark shades, poured an early morning shot of Wild Irish Rose and spoke his ultimate fantasy.

"I ought to build a hut right out there by Gracie Mansion," he said, cackling, and snorted the wine down.

Standing on the corner of Forsyth and Canal Streets, Slim cast a scornful eye at the activity across the street. That was where cops in blue, men in yellow helmets from the Department of Transportation, and a pack of press people were attending the razing of his shantytown home.

"It's a waste of taxpayers' money, harassing homeless people," he said. "We're not in anybody's way. We've been here 10 years. Why all of a sudden now?"

Slim came to the Hill, a jumble of wooden huts and one giant teepee, four years ago, when he got down on his luck.

"I'm not the kind of person who's going to let somebody tell me where to live, what to do, what time to get up and what to eat. I'm not an 'institutionalizable' individual. The shelter system is not for me. That's why I made my way out here."

None of the Hill people is institutionalizable. Talk to them, people with nicknames like Panama and Sammy, and they'll tell you how they tumbled out of their previous lives.

"Me and my wife couldn't get along, so I left," Panama, 49 and the father of six, told me. Then: "Me and my boss got into an argument and I left."

"I lost my apartment, Sammy said. Family problems."

The Hill people used to work regular jobs, and they still work at odd jobs—loading and unloading trucks in Chinatown, peddling fake designer watches, hustling soda cans, discarded furniture and old clothes. "I've got a nice watch right here for $20," Slim said, whipping a fake Seiko out of his pocket.

But it only takes some bad luck, combined with some messing up, to land you on the street. It takes a job to get an apartment, but to keep an apartment requires a certain adherence to rules. You have to do the same dull job every day, appease the boss, pay the rent on time, stay off the booze, be polite to the wife or husband. This can lull a truly free spirit into what feels like a coma.

To the Hill people, the rules of life were like a tightrope, and they kept falling off. In the shantytown they could be themselves. They built their huts, furnished them with beds and tables, hitched their TVs to a cable hanging from a lamppost, and hoisted an oil drum to make running water.

It wasn't Sutton Place, but at least nobody told you what to do.

For the most part, the Hill people didn't bother anybody, either. They kept to themselves and formed their own self-supporting community. But there were enough incidents to annoy other folks in the neighborhood and at City Hall—

several fires, including one in which a Hill-dweller died, and a shootout last week. And there was some drug activity, too.

There probably weren't any more fires or shootouts or drug sales on the Hill than there were in the rest of the Lower East Side, or on the Upper West Side for that matter. But the Hill people had signed no leases, held no deeds and paid no taxes. And let's face it, if a fire broke out and caused multiple casualties, the city could be blasted to hell for not having closed it sooner.

When it comes to the homeless, City Hall stands astride the chasm between a rock and a hard place. Homeless activists, rabid with indignation, demand a home for everybody now. A few go into city government, convinced they can solve the housing problem. They can't, and go slinking off to other jobs, leaving a new generation of activists to keep on raging.

"We have been doing outreach on that site for years," Michael Kharfen of the mayor's office said of the Hill. "We've found places for more than half the people believed to be originally on the site. We have provided services to nearly 80 people from the site and around that area."

But the Hill people snort at the word services, knowing that it means a bed in a shelter or a slot in a rehab program that makes you follow rules so you can get an apartment of your own. You can't blame them for spurning the shelters—and as for the programs, well, there's that freedom problem again.

"I don't use drugs and I don't drink, Panama told me. If I could get an apartment at a good reasonable rent, say $300 a month for a kitchenette, I would take it. But I haven't heard about anything like that."

The terrible fact is that in New York City, reasonably priced, clean, safe housing is like gold ore. The city tries to provide it for those who can't get it themselves; but whenever it does, it sets off a gold rush. The line of prospectors—the homeless, the ill-housed—now stretches halfway around the mountain.

So the true free spirits—like Sammy, Panama and Slim— migrate to places like the Hill. It looked sordid to some, but to them, it was home. And it was freedom.

Where would Slim sleep last night? I asked him. "To tell you the truth, I do not know," he said. "Maybe I'll ride the train all

184

night, so when people come get on in the morning I'll be lying there with my shoes off, with my feet stinking."

He chuckled at the thought of it, and downed another mouthful of wine.

Heidi Offers NY Therapy
AUGUST 11, 1993

The first time we met I was hunched over like an old woman.

I had slept all night in some unnatural position or another, and I woke up twisted like a pretzel, unable even to turn my head.

After that, there was a day of intense pain and a night of sleeping in an armchair, because it hurt too much to lie down. That sent me scurrying for someone who could make things right. She agreed to see me on a Saturday night.

This is how I fell into the healing hands of Heidi Fleiss. After 20 minutes on her couch I felt like a new woman. I could walk upright. I could turn my head without pain. Wow, that Heidi was something else!

Heidi Fleiss? The Hollywood Madam? The nymphet who has half the moguls in Hollywood quivering in the shadow of her little black book?

No, dear, I'm talking about the real Heidi Fleiss. Heidi of New York. My chiropractor.

When I phoned her yesterday she was just opening a letter. It began: "Dear Heidi . . . and I thought you were a chiropractor . . ."

It's been that way ever since her namesake broke into the news. People say, "I thought I really knew you." Or they call and plead, "Please, please don't let my name out of your appointment book! I'll pay you anything!"

Dr. Fleiss figures she and Hollywood Heidi are distant cousins. Fleiss, which is German for industrious, is a very rare name—and all the Fleisses who spell their name that way are related, Dr. Fleiss says.

But this is not the kind of notoriety Dr. Fleiss of New York's

Upper East Side was expecting when she was working her way through college, plus four years of chiropractic school. She describes chiropractic as the science and philosophy of relieving nerve irritation from the spine to allow the maximum flow of nerve energy through the body. This is done through adjustments of the body.

When I first went to see Dr. Fleiss, I was suffering from cervical neuritis, an inflammation of the neck and shoulder. In other words, my upper body was all bollixed up, and I could hardly move. Dr. Fleiss put me through a series of adjustments that reminded me of swimming lessons combined with resuscitations for someone who has almost drowned. When she got through with me, I could move again.

Often, when the pressure of writing has tied me into knots, I have returned to her office. One of my favorite adjustments is having my neck cracked. "The cracking sound," Dr. Fleiss explains, "is caused by the release of air that has built up in a joint that has irritation. When you release the pressure by gently jerking the neck, the air escapes." All I know is that it does clear my head.

When you do chiropractic work, it's kind of weird being confused with someone who's accused of being a prostitute. "It's pretty wild," Dr. Fleiss says. "When I see my name in this story, it's such an antithesis to what I could ever imagine myself being. I don't think anyone has confused her with me. Nobody would believe me if I told them I was a madam."

This week, a mob of journalists practically trampled Hollywood Heidi as she entered a Los Angeles courthouse to face pandering and cocaine charges. The daughter of a pediatrician (do doctors run in the family?), the willowy, mini-skirted Hollywood Heidi looked amused by all the publicity. The combination of illegal drugs, illicit sex and very rich people is as American as Valium—but for some reason, journalists freak out when they learn about a bona fide example of the three coming together.

Heidi Fleiss the chiropractor has gotten her share of publicity—a write-up a couple of years ago in New York Woman magazine and a small blurb in the current issue of Self. "But nobody has even seen the Self story," she sighed.

Dr. Fleiss shook me up for a moment when she told me she

has treated patients who come in complaining of sexual problems—such as not being able to get an erection, or having no sex drive.

Was Dr. Fleiss's chiropractic work in some way linked to Hollywood Heidi's brand of sexual healing, then?

"When they come in with an erection problem, sometimes it really is due to nerve irritation," Dr. Fleiss told me.

And how does she treat that, uh, condition, I asked?

"I do what's necessary. Sometimes it involves the lumbar nerve, the lower part of the spine above the sacrum . . ."

Aw, shucks, Dr. Fleiss!

Driving Racism
JANUARY 6, 1992

On the afternoon of December 15, 1989, Lillian Cannon, a Manhattan resident, hailed a yellow cab parked on the corner of East Houston and Ludlow Streets.

Mihai Surgent, the cab driver, was standing beside the driver's door when Cannon approached him and called "Taxi!" Surgent asked Cannon where she was going, and she motioned toward East River Drive. Surgent exploded. "No! No! No!" he yelled, refusing to take her.

Lillian Cannon is black.

While she was taking down the taxi's license plate number, two white women hailed the same cab and entered it without being questioned by Surgent about their destination. The cab took off, leaving Cannon behind on the sidewalk.

Cannon was one of the more fortunate ones. She filed a complaint against Surgent and the Wayside Cab Corp., owner of the cab, with the New York City Commission on Human Rights. Last October, Wayside agreed to pay Cannon $2,000 for the abuse she suffered and promised to distribute antidiscrimination information to its employees. The cab company has since gone out of business.

There was also the story of my friend Dellon Wilson, a quiet woman who also happens to be in the critical stages of aplastic anemia. Some months ago, she quarreled with a yellow cab driver who refused to take her to her destination. The driver threw Dellon out of the car onto the ground and hit her. Dellon, who receives regular blood transfusions for her illness, was injured and suffered a setback in her condition. Dellon is also black.

There's also my own story, or rather a pack of stories. I'll tell you two of them. took place several years ago as I tried to hail a cab on upper Broadway to take me to church on Sunday morning. A yellow cab stopped in front of me and I moved forward to open the door. The driver apparently thought he was stopping for the white couple standing next to me. When he saw me approach, he pulled away so fast the car skidded all over the street and almost ran through the red light.

After attending a Christmas Eve church service two weeks ago, I and others gathered on the corner of 120th Street and Broadway, trying to hail cabs to get home. We may have been suffused by the spirit of Christmas, but the cab drivers were not. One by one, the taxis passed me by, only to stop for the nearest white person three feet away. Finally, after all the whites were gone, a cab stopped for me.

I am not a columnist who constantly harps on the theme of racism. Unlike some black writers, I do not see a racist plot behind every slight or misfortune that befalls me. But I know this: If a person of color is ever tempted to forget that racism is alive and thriving in the world, all he or she has to do is try to hail a cab in New York City.

That's why I chuckled over Mayor David N. Dinkins' proposal last week to allow street hailing privileges to livery cabs—those cabs operated by private car services. Only yellow cabs currently have hailing privileges, and I am thrilled every time I hear of yellow cab drivers having their privileges eroded.

It is maddening and humiliating to be snubbed by a taxi and to realize it is a racial snub. Nothing is quite so basic and clear as having a cab go right past your furiously waving body and pick up the white person next to you. Sometimes you can debate whether racism was the motivating factor in an act; here there is no doubt whatsoever.

A 1987 study by the New York City Human Rights Commission, which sent out black and white decoys to flag down cabs, found that more than 60 percent of those passed up by cab drivers were black. The situation was worst on the Upper East Side and black men were the most likely to be passed by, but cab drivers pass black women in large numbers too.

In New York City it is illegal for a cab driver to refuse service because of a person's race or because of the client's requested destination. A cab driver is supposed to take a client where the client wants to go, not where the driver wants to take him. But the law is rarely enforced.

Last year, the Taxi and Limousine Commission received 937 complaints against cab drivers for refusal of service. Only 558 complainants followed through to the point of a hearing, and 459 cab drivers were convicted of refusing service. This does not take into account the thousands of cabs that whiz by persons of color so quickly and in such rapid succession that it's impossible to take down their license plates. Nor does it include the countless persons who are snubbed, but just don't bother to complain about it.

Last year, only 39 cab drivers had their license revoked, including 14 for refusing service or overcharging passengers.

The mayor's proposal does not extend to gypsies, that great unchartered fleet of 10,000 to 20,000 drivers who stick a livery sign on the window of their battered Fords and Pontiacs and go forth as cab drivers. But a word about gypsies. Given the choice, I'd rather ride in a metered cab, which means either a yellow cab or a cab owned by a private car service. With the gypsies you never know if you're riding with a recent parolee who has no car insurance and maybe not even a driver's license. And the physical conditions of some of the gypsy cabs I've ridden in has been deplorable.

But the fact is if it weren't for gypsies, people of color in this city would not be able to get taxis. I'm not talking about the small percentage of blacks and Latinos portrayed in the newspapers and on TV as thugs and robbers, who're just waiting to bop a cab driver over the head and take his money. I'm talking about the majority of blacks and Latinos in the city—the ones who work hard, pay their rent and mortgages, try to raise their children right, and are entitled to be treated with respect and civility.

I'm talking about the black and Latino maids and store clerks, security guards and bus drivers, cops and school-teachers, who're trying to get home to the Bronx, or Harlem or Brooklyn, often late at night, and are left stranded on the street corner by a succession of empty cabs.

Lillian Cannon was lucky. She got the cab driver's license and, in the end, a cash settlement, although the money cannot assuage the anger and humiliation that must still burn within her three years later.

My rational side says we must deal with this problem by encouraging everyone who can to report the offending cab drivers, to get their license numbers whenever possible, to follow up on the administrative hearings, to file complaints with the Human Rights Commission. And I urge the city to revoke more licenses of the offending drivers.

But my emotional side cries out too. And what it says is that every person of color ought to carry a gun and when a cab driver intentionally passes you by, you ought to blow out the tires on that sucker's car.

Jobless Numbers

AUGUST 26, 1991

Sometimes numbers tell the story better than any anecdote.

Take the numbers that sprang from the ashes of last week's rioting in Crown Heights. According to police, 91 arrests were processed between Tuesday and Thursday. These were people engaged in such behavior as throwing rocks and bottles, breaking windows, overturning cars, confronting cops and beating up people on the streets.

The overwhelming majority of those arrested were black males in their teens and early 20s. When asked by the police to give their occupations, of the 91 arrested, 63 said they had no occupation. Another 24 said their primary activity was something other than a job. This second category could include anything, from students to people who work sporadically. But it's the first number that concerns me.

It is possible that of the 63 arrestees who said they have no occupation, some simply didn't want to provide employment information for fear of losing their jobs. But these numbers make one thing pretty clear—that the majority of those rioting in Crown Heights last week were unemployed black men.

I figured this out on my own as I stood on the corner of Utica Avenue and President Street on Thursday afternoon, only hours after the worst spasm of rioting ended. Three nights before, 7-year-old Gavin Cato was struck and killed by a car driven by Yosef Lifsh, touching off the violence. Now, on every corner of the intersection stood a group of young black men who seemed to have nowhere else to go and nothing else to do.

I was there on Thursday as a member of the working press. The handful of cops who were guarding the intersection were there as members of the working police force. But what could explain the presence of so many young men standing on a street corner in the middle of the afternoon, unless they had no jobs to go to?

This is an all too familiar sight in New York City, and some more numbers are illustrative. According to national unemployment figures for the month of June, the unemployment rate for black men 16 to 19 years old was 37.4 percent, almost twice the rate for white men of the same age (19.9 percent). The unemployment rate for black women 16 to 19 years old was second-highest (28.9 percent), twice as high as that for white women in the same category (14.9 percent). Consider that these figures represent people who are unemployed and actively looking for work, and don't include those who have given up, and the actual percentage of black men and women who are without jobs reaches staggering proportions.

Consider some more numbers. In New York City, during the first six months of this year, only 66,000 of the 430,000 young people between the ages of 16 and 19 (of all races) were gainfully employed. While 50 percent of teenagers nationwide—in cities like Peoria, Ill., Phoenix, and San Antonio—were either working or actively looking for work, three-quarters of New

York City youths were doing neither. In this city legions of young people are idle.

"They are," says Samuel Ehrenhalt, regional commissioner of the federal Bureau of Labor Statistics, "the unemployed, the underemployed, and the not even unemployed (because the notion of working is foreign to them), young men who are just drifting and are completely outside the mainstream of the job scene."

The simple truth about Crown Heights, and Bensonhurst, and Astoria, just about any other neighborhood you can name, is that people with jobs don't riot. They have too much to lose— their livelihoods, homes, cars, the education for their children, their stake in the future—by running wild in the streets. Only those who have nothing else to do are free to vent their frustration and pent-up energy on the persons and property of others.

Being unemployed is not an excuse for breaking windows or breaking heads. But it is one of the main causes of such behavior. If those young black men in Crown Heights had been at their jobs last Tuesday and Wednesday nights, or at home preparing for the next day's work, they wouldn't have been creating mayhem in the streets.

We have known this for decades, certainly since the riots of the 1960s, and yet we do nothing about it. The federal government no longer makes even a token effort to create jobs for the legions of the chronically unemployed. President George Bush may look up from his golf swing long enough to ponder a coup d'etat in the Soviet Union, but not long enough to observe the idleness of the young men and women in America's cities.

Businesses bemoan the situation, but are not acting aggressively to provide jobs for this segment of the population. And public schools, which have proven the value of exposing students to work through cooperative work-study programs, are doing far less in this area than they should. Currently, 12,000 public school children have part-time jobs because the schools, in conjunction with local businesses, have created jobs for them. How much better a city this would be if that number were 50,000 or 100,000.

Moreover, black parents and the leadership in black communities are not doing enough to encourage black youths to take whatever work is available, however menial and unglamorous, and to use that experience as a steppingstone to better jobs and an alternative to idleness and crime.

The numbers from Crown Heights make it plain: People with jobs don't riot. If we want livable neighborhoods, we have to put people to work.

Flair in a Gray City
DECEMBER 13, 1989

In her photograph, she is aristocratic and alluring, a young woman in her twenties with jet-black hair, high cheekbones and a stunning smile. She sits on a table in full Mexican dress—a sweeping skirt, a long, colorful shawl, or rebozo, draping her shoulders, and a huge sombrero. Massive earrings frame her pretty face.

This was the picture of Juanita Garcia on display recently in a back room of the Mexican Consulate on East 41st Street. The picture sat in the middle of her ofrenda, a sort of shrine to the dead.

Garcia's shrine was a circus of objects. Artificial flowers, decorative beads, candles, carved animals, mirrors in silver frames, all laid out on tables of different heights. According to Mexican folklore, it takes four years for a dead person to reach the netherworld, and these objects are, symbolically, provisions for the journey. There was fruit, a glass of water, a bottle of mescal (liquor made from the cactus plant), and lots of toy skulls and skeletons. An ofrenda is also a way of mocking death.

Among the thousands of deaths each year in this city and the many ways of expressing grief, this one was unusual. Its outpouring of symbols seemed so flamboyant that I wanted to learn more about this woman who had apparently touched so many people. So I asked her friends, including Juan May, a retired toolmaker, and Rudy Leal, a computer specialist. Both of them met her through the Centro Mexicano de Nueva York, a Mexican cultural group.

When Juanita Garcia died last April at about 79 (her exact

193

age is unknown), she had been in New York City for 57 years. One of thousands of Mexicans who streamed into the country in the '20s when immigration laws were less strict, she crossed legally into Texas in 1924, when she was about 14. Little is known about her family, but it is clear that she was alone. After working as a maid in Los Angeles for eight years, she moved east to New York.

"I met her in 1937," May said. "Our group started as a joke and then it got serious and we realized it was a must. The president of the group said, 'Well, Juan, here's another paisan who is going to help us.'"

May found her a real patriot, someone who loved Mexico and actively sought out her compatriots. She used to go and visit the illegals and help them out and give them money, May said.

In New York, she led a life of contrasts. She found work as a domestic, working in the rectory of St. Patrick's Cathedral and for 13 years as a maid at the Salvation Army women's residence on East 29th Street. She lived in a rented room on West End Avenue. She became a naturalized U.S. citizen. And while she had boyfriends, she did not marry or have children.

Juanita Garcia's life did not seem glamorous to the people she worked with. "She was a very nice, friendly, hard-working lady," recalls Cora Jacobs, head housekeeper of the Salvation Army's Anthony residence, who was Garcia's boss for 9 years. "She kept to herself. She didn't talk much about her personal life."

But away from the job, her life blossomed in the presence of her Mexican friends. They got together at Centro Mexicano meetings at the McBurney YMCA on West 23rd Street, where they shared memories of home.

Among her friends, the quiet maid became the flamboyant senorita. She wore high heels and fringed capes dripping with costume jewelry. Tall and thin, she entered rooms with a flourish. She dyed her hair black until her death, and she loved to dance, to teach folk dances to Mexican children.

"To me she was the most Mexican of my group," says Leal, who met Garcia just two years ago. "She had a certain air about her."

Garcia's goal was to teach non-Mexicans about her own

culture. She brought whites and blacks to the Centro. She bought a whole sound system for the Ballet Folkorico of New York so they could rehearse.

"She was the flag-bearer of our group, which meant she had to know the history of the flag. She was always the one to bring coffee to Centro meetings. At one of the last meetings she attended, she made Mexican chocolate, which burned in the coffee pot, so the coffee tasted like rubber."

During World War II, she had worked as a barmaid, entertaining sailors with stories of her homeland. One of her prized possessions was a Nazi armband, believed to be a memento given her by a sailor friend. Her birthday was as elusive as her age. She gave many different dates, including May 5, Mexican Independence Day.

Two years ago, Garcia had to retire, and began to go in and out of the hospital with mysterious ailments that she declined to discuss with friends. She stopped coming to Centro's meetings. Last April, a member of the group went to Garcia's home to tell her about an upcoming event, only to be told by the landlord that she had died.

Leal traced her body to the morgue. Police said she died of natural causes, that she had laid in her room for days before being found. Leal had to identify her decomposed body by her hair and cheekbones.

Last April, Garcia's friends held a Mexican-style wake for her at a Manhattan funeral home. A hundred people led by a Catholic priest chanted prayers for her. The next day her friends—Mexicans, whites, the black domestics who worked with her—attended a mass at Our Lady of Guadalupe Church. Even people who were archenemies at Centro Mexicano set aside their differences for the occasion.

The church donated a funeral plot in Woodside, Queens, and Juanita Garcia was buried there on May 1, four days before her native country's independence day. Friends went to her home and found many trappings of her life: huge, fringed capes, loads of costume jewelry, costumes of all kinds. And there were her savings of more than $90,000, which, because she left no will, and has no known relatives, will probably go to the state.

Her friends have ordered a simple granite tombstone with a

carving of Our Lady of Guadalupe, the patron saint of Mexico. They plan to visit her grave next April, on the anniversary of her death.

Garcia was not an important person. She was a Mexican woman who made New York City her home. She worked hard. She lived most of her days in rented rooms. And she spread the love of her culture to others who wouldn't otherwise have learned about it.

She was one of the ordinary people one passes on the street or in the subway, on her way to clean the rooms of others. But to her friends, Juanita Garcia's life was a flash of color, brightening the grayness of the city.

The Garden Is Still Green

AUGUST 30, 1993

In a once-abandoned lot between a homeless shelter and the FDR Drive, Noe Perez dashed through a sweltering noon and led me to his melon patch.

"That one is almost ready," Perez said, pointing to a cantaloupe nestled among sunflowers, yellow corn, and a shady covering of weeds.

"This took patience," he said. "This took a lot of time."

Perez' patch is one of many such patches carved out of this urban garden on East 29th Street behind Bellevue Hospital Center. Here, all manner of fruits and vegetables and plants with magical names like lemon balm, chamomile and foxglove grow behind fences made of discarded metal bedposts plucked from the garbage.

The garden is as wild as New York City, and as messy in places as the lives of the 40 or so men who tend it. They are alcoholic outpatients at Bellevue Hospital, and tending the garden is part of their therapy.

Perez, 51, worked for 20 years as a time-clock mechanic, but he kept on drinking liquor until the job and two marriages fell apart. Now he weeds his garden, waters his melons and watches his flowers grow.

196

"If you just get a seat in the shade and watch these flowers, how they grow and cling to life, that's an inspiration. It makes you cling to life too."

On a day when the mayor of the city was being deposed about alleged crimes against Jews, when a blind sheik sat in a jail cell awaiting the public's retribution, and city employees scraped mounds of asbestos out of public schools, Noe Perez' garden said more about life in this city than any of the madness that was in the headlines.

This garden in the crack of nowhere is one of thousands of secret gardens around the city where people are going about their business—coping, recovering, taking small steps day by day, tending to their lives the way Perez tends his melons. A city with enough people like these cannot die.

Michele Hurley, 32, a former housewife from Brooklyn, is one of them. Two years ago, her husband was beaten up by muggers, then lost his job as a subway conductor because he was out of work for more than a year. The Hurleys and their four kids were forced to go on welfare. A letter from the city's Department of Employment offered to train her for a job. Hurley signed up at one of the city's Testing Assessment and Placement (TAP) centers, got 16 weeks of training at The Brooklyn Hospital Center, and for the past eight months has been working as a geriatric nursing technician at Brooklyn Hospital. The Hurley family is no longer on welfare.

On the day I was offered a slice of Noe Perez' watermelon, police officer Ralph Gengo of Staten Island got his detective's badge after 11 years on the police force. To accomplish this, Gengo, 38, slogged his way through five years on motor patrol, four years in undercover work and 18 more months chasing down robbers in order to earn his shield.

"I always wanted to be a detective," Gengo told me. "There's no other police department like the NYPD. It's fast, it's quick. It's the toughest job in New York. When most people run away from trouble, we're running toward it. That's the difference between a police officer and a civilian."

You look at Perez, Hurley and Gengo, and realize that New York City is not nearly as bad as it's made out to be. Granted, we have a school system that squanders 14 years and millions of dollars on a scam asbestos-removal program. But the same school system this year graduated students who won $147 million in college scholarships, and the same system will open up 32 small, new, innovative high schools this fall. These are the first new general public high schools in 20 years.

This is the city that served 12 million meals to senior citizens last year, that paid the rent increases for thousands of poor residents, and provided home care to 150,000 elderly people. There are so many more services for the elderly in New York City that some are moving here from places like Florida and South Carolina because their quality of life is better here.

New York may have the most obnoxious team in baseball, but for every Vince Coleman who is bounced from his job there is a Michele Hurley, who is trained by a city program to support her family. Last year, 48,000 adults and 59,000 kids got jobs or job training through the city.

None of the tragedies or scandals of this city elude us, but they have nothing to do with a woman getting off welfare, a cop earning a promotion, or an alcoholic who finds renewal by tending a garden.

This brings me back to Noe Perez' garden. He works here three to four hours a day, watering the plants, pulling weeds, carrying away soil and debris. Perez' feet are bad and his joints hurt, the legacy of years of drinking. But he sits here in the shade on a milk crate and finds relief.

At the center of the garden on East 29th Street is an upended willow tree, lying on its side with its huge roots exposed. It was toppled during a snowstorm last winter, but the gardeners chose to leave it as it is. Like the city, the tree is ravaged, but is still growing, and all around it are patches of great beauty.